F   270

1-1941.

Massachusetts Beautiful

Massachusetts Beautiful

BY
WALLACE NUTTING

ILLUSTRATED BY THE AUTHOR WITH THREE
HUNDRED AND FOUR PICTURES COVERING
ALL THE COUNTIES IN MASSACHUSETTS

BONANZA BOOKS · NEW YORK

This edition published by Bonanza Books,
a division of Crown Publishers, Inc.
f g h

Manufactured in the United States of America

FOREWORD

THE author's book on Vermont in this series of the States Beautiful covered largely a virgin field. It will at once occur to many that a new book on Massachusetts will with difficulty establish its right to exist. It is true that a great many illustrated books have been issued on the old houses and haunts of Massachusetts. However, there still remain numerous picturesque cottages which have never been shown in any volume. Even some of the stately houses have not been depicted except externally. The interior of a good house is or ought to be far more interesting than the exterior.

There has not, however, at any time, so far as we are aware, been an effort to set forth the picturesque landscapes of the state in extensive fashion. If one gathered up all the old wood cuts of Massachusetts scenery he would have a large and meritorious collection. Nearly all the pictures in this book are now published in book form for the first time and most of them are entirely new.

The effort to cover the entire state in a series of pictures of this sort does indeed lay one open to the charge that he has treated the subject too briefly. It is like finding fault with a clergyman for making his sermon too short, and must be taken as a compliment.

Two main ideas have been kept in mind in the preparation of this book. The first idea is that of avoiding any appreciable encroachment on what appears in other works. The second idea is to place before the public scenes with which they are not generally familiar but which merit attention.

It has seemed entirely inappropriate to refer at length to historical matters. Pictures of a very few famous localities are included, but history is left to the abundant works on the subject.

Little should be looked for of literary merit in a work of this kind. If the text is understandable, the reader will kindly consider that he has value received in the pictures. The text must necessarily aim chiefly at the description of the localities shown, and to such experiences or incidents as are connected therewith.

A desire expressed by many that pictures should be titled has been met in this volume and will be met in volumes which we hope will follow. From a very wide experience in titling pictures the author is persuaded that not one person in a multitude can find from its title the spot pictured. The author finds it difficult to get the exact viewpoint a second time.

It is a pleasure to a reader to know that a certain composition was found in his home town, whether or not he recognizes the spot. Of course, these remarks do not apply to features like mountains but they apply to almost every other composition.

Having spent some years in each one of the New England States the author feels at home in all of them.

The author has personally found and pictured all the themes set forth in this work. This originality of theme is not maintained to be a merit but it does set forth the subject in a fresh way.

It is true that many delightful scenes depicted by others might have been obtained for this book. The time may come when it will be found desirable to engage collaborators in this series, but in the present work the author is entirely responsible for all defects.

WALLACE NUTTING

Framingham
Massachusetts

To

THE MEMORY OF
THE FOUNDERS OF MASSACHUSETTS
WHOSE VISION, PERSISTENCE
AND DEVOTION TO IDEALS
ARE THEIR NOBLEST BEQUEST
TO US, THEIR CHILDREN

Massachusetts Beautiful

. .

MASSACHUSETTS

MASSACHUSETTS! A word surrounded with an aura of hope! A state with a soul! There is gathered up into her name the brilliant program of a new world. Her name summons before us a procession of benignant faces, their eyes filled with faith when first they gazed on her shores. She is the only state founded on an ideal, built on a principle. She is the state where character came in before cash and where men united for freedom but not for conquest. Her sons, foremost to give their blood for their own independence, were also foremost again to give it for the freedom of the slave. Small in area, great in influence, there is not a hill within her borders but calls to memory an action which dignifies human nature; not a stream but carries to the sea the moral and mental current of truth embellished by learning. Here Bradford prayed, Edwards taught, Warren fought! Each gave his heart and his brain to humanity. The sound judgment of Endicott and Hopkins and an innumerable company of prophets, sages, soldiers, to the day of Andrew, Webster and Sumner, have laid their talents on the altar of their country.

Her fair domain is not an unworthy field for her glory. Where gleams there an island-studded bay more safe and inviting than that of Massachusetts? Where opens a fairer valley or one richer in the bounty of the earth than that of the Connecticut, as seen in all its sweet

7

expanse from the summit of Mount Tom? Where are the hills more fragrant with blossoms than in the heart of her commonwealth, or more splendid with October glory than in the Berkshires? On what shores do the breakers surge with more of majesty or the sea wrinkle with more luring beauty than on Cape Ann and Cape Cod? Is there a stream where spindles hum more steadily than on the Merrimac, or where paper rolls out to feed the presses of our literature more generously than on the Housatonic and the Connecticut? Is there any other similar area where so many inventions for benignant use have been brought to perfection as in Massachusetts?

What village speaks more for developed human character than Concord? What center in the Nineteenth Century in America held so much of teeming intellectual life as that at the mouth of the Charles? Are there any hospitals nobler than hers, any legislatures that have originated so much of love embodied in law to shield the lives of women and children?

We cannot deny that the defects of our incomplete nature have left their scars on the history of Massachusetts, and that she has shared with humanity some touch of its bigotry, some fire of its baser passion. But in this state no decade has been without a host of witnesses for truth, for faith, for learning and for sacrifice. She has never lacked competence in leadership nor does she now. The men of Massachusetts have ever wanted to know and to do. They have learned. They have achieved. In every state of America there are laws and institutions and inspirations which, born here, have gone on with irresistible growth and developed potency to become the strength of America.

Massachusetts is worthy of our love; her history deserves our reverent study. She supplies an adequate theater for a greater development of mind and soul than has yet been attained.

Her stimulating climate, her well-watered slopes, her varied ocean shores, her strategic location, her resources in trained men are the fitting basis for a satisfactory future. But her proud heritage of victory over

CHRISTMAS EXPECTANCY

the obstacles of the flesh and the spirit, the heritage of truths tested, lifted and established in power and beauty, are a richer and more faithful prophecy of the Massachusetts that is to be.

MASSACHUSETTS BEAUTIFUL

THE stranger entering Massachusetts, especially if he comes from the western states, too often thinks of the Bay State as a region notable indeed historically but limited in scenic interest, or, if at all excellent in landscapes, to be so chiefly in the Berkshires.

Fashion plays a much larger part in the matter of travel than it has any right to assume. To the writer, the heart of the commonwealth in

Worcester County has in its orchards and streams more beauty perhaps than the Berkshires themselves. It is remarkable that the orchard districts of most states are nearly unknown to tourists. They are situated in fertile regions not noted as tourists' resorts. But as beautiful farm land desirable for the practical farmer, who is defined as one who takes his money out of the land, and to the agriculturist, who is defined as one who puts his money in, the gentle slopes of Grafton, Berlin, Bolton and Harvard and the fair plains of Lancaster, are thoroughly satisfactory. Groton, which was the original seat of the author's family, of course appeals to him. All about North Andover there is a beautiful district. Mention is made of these regions because there does not exist in any of them, perhaps, a famous seasonal resort.

Cape Cod, indeed, has appealed very strongly to many, more particularly since it came so much under the public eye as the scene of literary effort. Mrs. Hemans speaks of the Pilgrims landing " on a stern and rock-bound coast." While any shore is stern in time of storm, the " south shore " of Massachusetts, at least beyond Cohasset, is seldom bold and perhaps never rocky. There are those, indeed, who think that Plymouth Rock is kept under a canopy because rocks are so rare in its region. The remark has been made, based we believe on the United States Coast Survey, that after one leaves the cliffs in the vicinity of Gloucester there are no bold crags on the Atlantic coast all the way to Mexico with the exception of those found at Watch Hill, Rhode Island. The author hopes he may never be compelled to follow this entire distance and he, therefore, is under the necessity of quoting. In a general way it may be said that Maine monopolizes, with a small share grudged to Massachusetts, nearly all the boldly picturesque Atlantic coast.

We find, then, in glorious old Massachusetts a good variety of sea, mountain and meadow. She has aspects which win all her faithful children, some of whom are now in every quarter of the wide American domain and, indeed, in every part of the earth.

A NOOK IN PLYMOUTH

THE GARFIELD HOMESTEAD—LINCOLN

There is an inspirational effect in touring Massachusetts because back of its beauty lies its quaintness, its romance, its ideals and the glory of standing for the first great experiment in a free and expansible principle of government. People come from the West and the South and stand, often with uncovered heads, at the patriotic shrines of this state, feeling that hence sprung those virile, germinal ideas, which, shot through the entire fabric of national life, make it mean more than the life of any other nation. It is impossible to separate the sense of beauty from the sense of the past, giving a halo to every landscape. Howsoever gloomy the day there is an ancient hidden fire discernible pulsating through the atmosphere and always a rainbow of hope. For here, if the ideals of Massachusetts prove immortal, will be an enduring and uplifted human society. And here, if those ideals must die, how glorious will be their burial place! As in Holland the flattest landscape and the tamest material surroundings often thrill us with the memory of the contests of those sturdy people, so here every old roadside is eloquent with the echoes of ancient marches to liberty and light and power.

We need not confine ourselves to the historic route of Paul Revere in order to move along amidst challenges to memory and beckonings to nobler living. On many hundreds of miles of her beautiful highways there are, here and there, edifices which embody ennobling events, or granite memorials of a past which never lived as vitally as now. It is true that some old states seem to have outlived their history. But are not these instances where there was never a really free people, as in Egypt and Mesopotamia? Wherever human life has struck the high and fine note the spirit of the fathers seems never to depart. From the Acropolis and from the Forum we can never miss the glorious shades that have stood for something fine and strong and helpful in human nature.

Still less in this dear state of our birth, a state now starting on its fourth century of civilization, can we ever get away from the history that inspires us.

We look forward to the time, we believe not far distant, when patriotic societies, or the state itself, shall restore and mark appropriately all those homes or scenes where bold and far-seeing men have taken advance ground and given to us new standards of thought and action.

CAPE COD

THE residents of Plymouth and vicinity are particular to make it plain to the traveler that Cape Cod does not begin until we reach the canal. The contour of Cape Cod and what one sees there are always a surprise to the visitor on his first journey. These notable aspects of surprise may be mentioned: in the first place, although Cape Cod is narrow and runs away into the sea, one may journey the length of the Cape and seldom see the ocean. In part this is owing to the necessity of keeping a through route away from the inlets in order to secure a reasonable directness; in part it is due to the hills; but in part it seems a mystery.

The second surprise awaiting the strange visitor lies in the extremely hilly nature of the Cape. We are almost ready to say that it is the hilliest part of Massachusetts. This notably uneven contour adds much to the charm of the Cape, which one would otherwise find monotonous. Of course the hills being no more than huge dunes are the effect of wind and sea, but some of them have great height. One would hardly suppose the elements were so powerful as to create such a contour. But it is well known that since the settlement of Massachusetts small estuaries which enabled one to sail through a canal across the narrow portion of the Cape have silted up. Again, at Chatham the great bluff has been eaten into by the fierce seas so that within our life-time lighthouses have been removed to safer foundations. This is stranger inasmuch as many shoals off the eastern part of the Cape would seem to compel the sea to tame its wrath. We remember with a shudder even now that the May-

RIVER GROWTHS—HARDING

PLEASANT BAY CREEK—ORLEANS

ALL IN A GARDEN FAIR—FRAMINGHAM

flower came near foundering in the unknown shallows east of the Cape in her effort to round it and reach " Virginia." The captain put back because he felt that his position was altogether too hazardous, and therefore Provincetown became the first landing place.

The third surprising feature of the Cape is its numerous and large fresh water ponds. These ponds nestling at the foot of sharp dunes are objects of great beauty, especially as the pond lily, either by nature or cultivation, often spreads its beauty in their coves. Some of these ponds are of great size; some are divided from the sea by a mere low sand dike. The water is generally delicious and pure. In this particular Cape Cod is only exceeded by the region around Plymouth.

It is useless to follow Thoreau after his classical description of a journey to Cape Cod. There are, however, many who challenge various conclusions of his and the native does not regard him at all with favor. Probably the most striking phrase in his volume is that in which he says that the Cape Codder ploughs the ocean and his plough is moved by a white sail.

It is eminently true that whatever prosperity the Cape used to enjoy arose from the wealth of the sea and the industries which were allied with fisheries and commerce.

An agreeable sleepiness which we trust may not be disturbed pervades some of the old villages, though these same villages would probably resent being thought somnolent. Their somnolence is their charm because the traveler does or should seek rest, and there is a fine aroma about a quiet old village by the sea not comparable to or equalled by other haunts. Aroma as here used refers to the spiritual essence and not to the fishy odors which we do not otherwise mention, but we could, oh, we could!

Provincetown itself has of late, indeed, been seized by a new band of Pilgrims, the Portuguese who succeeded the Yankee in the fisheries, and who now themselves are finding other lines of effort more attractive. One finds himself as much in a foreign land, as is possible here in America, in Provincetown, in spite of the lofty monument which commemorates the first landing of our fathers.

The finest attractions connected with Provincetown are her back yards, her sea gardens as one may say, where the rollicking hollyhocks hold undisputed sway, towering over their humbler floral neighbors. There are little lanes and alleys and nooks loved by the artist and sought out by the tourist where the flowers, seeming to get a permanence of beauty by the seaside, are allowed full scope. It has probably been remarked a great many times that the near influence of the sea is very favorable to floral development, giving it a brightness and a longevity of blossom quite superior to that of flowers grown in the interior. This effect is seen all along as one comes down from Boston.

There is something good to be said for the Portuguese which is not so marked in the natives of Cape Cod. These natives are quiet and reserved, following the more usual habit of the English people. The Portuguese are rather notably courteous and lively and have added a note of joyousness and vivacity which may be more superficial than the sturdy graces of the English character, but is, nevertheless, agreeable as met by the traveler.

The fine summer air of the forearm of the Cape affords an escape from the severe heats of the interior which is scarcely inferior to the same relief afforded by Nantucket. The land is here so narrow that the climate is essentially insular and free from the extremes which are so trying in America.

It has become a chronic habit to joke about the barren soil of the Cape; to say that it is so poor that one cannot raise an umbrella on it, and to indulge in all sorts of jibing or contemptuous remarks regarding its sands. It is found, however, that certain flowers and produce if well fed by artificial means come to a fine maturity and flavor on the Cape. There are also streaks here and there on the lower lands of fair loam which can hardly be surpassed for many sorts of cultivation. Thus, though the dominant feature may be sand, there is, what with the use

AN APPLE-ELM CURVE—HARVARD

PLEASANT BAY—ORLEANS

A BELCHERTOWN MARGIN

A WEYMOUTH HOLLYHOCK DOOR

THE POOL AT SANDWICH, CAPE COD

of the sandy sites for summer cottages, and the use of the better soil for crops, no small opportunity for much larger development on the Cape than has hitherto existed.

Some portions of the Cape have gone backward and that to a very great extent, there being a lonely aspect to certain of the districts which formerly harbored a considerable number of bold fishermen, nor is this to be regretted. On the other hand a great many sections of the Cape have developed to an extent far beyond anything in their previous history. The Cape stands out as the only readily accessible portion of our shores where summer mildness is obtainable. It has been said with probable truth that had not the winter of the Pilgrims' landing been mild the entire enterprise connected with the Mayflower would have perished and with it the fine moral stimulus which they, in the course of Providence, imparted to our continent.

Provincetown was the point whence they explored southerly, and they found even then that the Indians, who from the crudeness of their civilization were obliged to take advantage of every superficial source of supply, had their scattered habitations on this portion of the Cape. Provincetown is a delightful sail from Boston and like all termini has a certain emphatic effect upon the traveler's memory. It is an agreeable prowling place for those sated with the usual.

Moving southward along the forearm of the Cape one finds in the rolling hills of Truro a certain romantic lift and stimulus to dream of the strenuous past. Off this shore innumerable wrecks have brought to an end many a career and have tossed up, still clinging to life, many a denizen of other regions to take up, in this precarious manner, his new career in America.

Now that the Cape Cod canal is in operation, coastwise shipping no longer has an incentive to hug the shoals of the Cape and we may hope, what with the lighthouses and the experiences of the past, that generations to come will escape the fearful wrecks which are the most dominant thought in one's mind as he wanders along these treacherous shores.

CAPE COD COTTAGES

THE Cape Cod cottage has achieved the distinction of receiving this specific name. There are many thousands of houses of precisely the same type scattered through New England but this cottage is so uniformly found at the Cape that we take no issue with the appellation. The stranger at Cape Cod is often puzzled by the term " double house." In the Cape Cod significance this phrase refers to a house with a chimney in the middle and a room on both sides. Frequently the space on either side of the chimney is divided into more than one room. Of course, the term " double house " used elsewhere of a dwelling for two families, confuses the stranger. The name arose on Cape

A BARRE BROOK

A PETERSHAM WOODLAND

AN OLD DANVERS HOME ROOM

Cod from the fact that the first settler built a tiny house with the chimney at one end and with perhaps a front and rear room downstairs, the rear room being a small bedroom opening off the kitchen. This is called a "single house." The addition of a duplication of the structure on the other side of the chimney gives the local significance of the "double house."

These dwellings are uniformly of one story in height although they are often erroneously called one and a half stories, as they have, generally, two rooms in the attic. The eaves, however, rise directly above the first floor, as a rule, without any side wall on the second story. Further, these houses are almost always shingled. Where they are left unpainted, as is usually the case, they acquire a beautiful gray which cannot be distinguished from the stone walls found before one reaches the Cape where such houses also appear. This gray effect is the result of intimacy with the weather and requires some years to reach its perfection. In many instances white paint has been applied to these houses and never with aesthetic advantage. The dweller within the cottage may indeed protect his dwelling and feel that he has a trimmer anchorage with a painted house, but he loses that mellow melting into the atmosphere, and that nameless charm of roof and side wall in the same natural tint.

No possible preparation of the shingle can give an artificial color matching this superb gray. Furthermore, the side wall of a house will last for generations without paint. The "John Alden" house at Duxbury has some of the original side shingles applied about 1663. It is true they are getting to need some repairs! Of course the old shingles were often made of shaved pine which render them almost eternal. The sawed shingle catches and holds the water whereas the shaved shingle sheds it.

There is a remarkable absence of gambrel roofs on Cape Cod. The author was informed that there were none whatever on the Cape. It was with some glee, therefore, that he discovered a very ancient gambrel roof in Chatham, but he admits that it is the only one that he has seen.

The usual Cape Cod cottage is very simple but has a winning quality. Persons of wealth sometimes construct such cottages. If they are erected so that two or even three cottages meet each other by a lap wide enough for a door, the effect is very excellent and one has the advantage of all possible light and air. In such a case the attic may be left in the rough and soon becomes the receptacle of all sorts of useless but delightful lumber.

The Cape Cod cottage at its best should have a large chimney. Unfortunately the reasonless craze for improvement has resulted in the destruction of such chimneys in many instances and the erection of shabby, spindling affairs under the alleged excuse of getting more room within the cottage. Of course this means the abolition of the old fireplaces. Even if a new chimney is erected there is no reason for drawing it down to so minute a dimension since to do so takes away all dignity from the house. We cannot enough deplore the hateful and tasteless arrangement of a wooden frame work around some chimneys in recent construction to give the effect of size. This work is false to art, to taste, to sentiment and to reason.

These old chimneys sometimes have a rounded top to keep out the weather as is the case with one shown in this book. More often, however, they were left so that the storm might beat in. This fault may be overcome by placing a stone set up at the corners over the chimney so as to permit egress of smoke if one does not care to take the trouble to construct the arch.

The Cape Cod house is further characterized in its best form by three minute windows on each end in the gable, one on each side under the eaves lighting the long closets in the otherwise useless space divided off from the attic room, and the third at the point of the gable, ventilating the dead air space over the attic room. These little windows, invariably with four lights of glass, are sometimes called " dog house windows."

STOCKBRIDGE

A CORNER IN CHINA—NANTUCKET

ADAMS

QUEEN OF MAY—ASHFIELD

A lady of our acquaintance in trying to recall the name referred to them as " little dog windows."

In rare instances, the excellent architectural feature of a slight overhang on a line with the eaves, on the gable end, gives the house a great deal of added beauty and dignity. The front doors of these houses do not have head room permitting an elliptic light but semi-occasionally there is a line of low transom sash. In the best examples of earlier houses the window frames are well set out, being constructed of solid sizeable joists pinned together and enhancing the good lines of the dwelling.

Within, of course, there is a substantial fireplace on each side of the chimney in the double house, which greatly preponderates. In the rear there is sometimes a lean-to, although there is very little room to run a roof down, as the eave line is already low. In any case, however, there is sometimes in the rear a small kitchen and a third fireplace on that side of the chimney.

The front door opens into a small square entry formerly called the porch, and there is a narrow, steep stair running sidewise across the face of the chimney.

A cottage such as we have described, if it still has a stone wall or a post and rail fence about it, or even a picket fence, a few shade trees, and if it stands back somewhat from the street, is a very good example of the sort of home which meets all human need and possibly may be looked forward to as a future possession of every family, even the poorest. Meantime, it appeals to persons of the best taste as a desirable summer residence and by its unpretentious merits and simple beauty is in a way to teach us the quiet life.

Occasionally in the larger towns of the Cape, especially as one gets back toward the shoulder of the arm, we see the conventional two story house. Some of these are of a very excellent type, as in Brewster, Yarmouth and Sandwich. Such a house shows adjoining the church across the pool in the little sketch called " The Pond at Sandwich."

For those who are somewhat ambitious or are so thoroughly wonted to a sizeable house as not to be satisfied with the Cape Cod cottage, these last mentioned towns and others, as Hyannis and Falmouth, offer very attractive residences even for the whole year. The snows upon the Cape are not so deep as are found inland and winter motoring is less often interfered with. There is, to be sure, more wind even in this quarter of the Cape than farther inland, but compensating advantages are found.

VEGETATION ON THE CAPE

THE trees of the Cape as we first enter it from the west are in many cases noble elms shading the villages with dignity and spreading arching beauty. As we journey eastward the elms become very rare and the characteristic shade tree of the Cape is the poplar. We seldom see such noble poplars as seem to flourish here. It is very common to see rows of them before cottages. Evidently the soil is well adapted to their growth. Another tree unusual elsewhere is called the Tree of Heaven. It is uncommon even on the Cape. If you look at a blue china plate of the common willow ware you see this tree reaching over the waters where the runaway couple is hastening across. The foliation and the small branches remind one somewhat of the locust. At first glance it is often mistaken for that tree. It is probable that seedlings were brought from China by some of the old captains. The possession of such a tree, especially if of dignified size, gives a Cape Cod cottage a singular distinction.

The prevailing winds have governed all trees well out on the Cape, and they slant to leeward. This is the more remarkable as there are, it is to be presumed, prevailing winds far inland but this effect is seldom seen except on the shores.

There is little need to call particular attention to other vegetation on the Cape perhaps more than elsewhere except as relates to the small fruits already hinted at. On one occasion as we wound along a by-road

A DECORATED PINE—DUXBURY

THE MAJOR BRADFORD HOUSE—JONES RIVER

A HYANNIS BYWAY

A PROVINCETOWN BACK YARD

BROADWAY, NANTUCKET

we came upon a neat cottage worthy of portrayal. As we skirted about it we discovered the most luscious and wonderful cultivated blackberries we have ever seen. They were at the acme of perfection and we look back to the hour as that in which we exhibited a marked degree of Christian fortitude. With mouths watering and fingers itching, with no one looking, and even the cottage locked and everyone absent, was it not a mark of a deep-down religion which prevented our even tasting? How we wanted to try those berries! " 'Twere worth ten years of peaceful life one *quart* of their array! " But we didn't, we didn't! But whether as much character would assert itself in us again we are entirely uncertain.

The vegetation of the Cape is not particularly early. The sea holds back the spring just as it holds off the autumn and tends to equalize the seasons but the fruits and flowers are wonderfully attractive. Of late, also, certain areas are being exploited commercially with rye.

The water growths of the Cape are strikingly attractive. All about the margins of salt lagoons there are lovely grasses, and by the brook sides and wherever lowlands encourage water to lie, the tall reeds with their blossoms or their cattails, according to the season, form artistic borders. By a cottage near a brook where children played as seen on these pages we lingered with them by the hour. The clear sand, the luscious high swaying reeds, the near-by cottage door where the housewife sang, the mellow sunlight and the little bridge by the side of which a turn-out for watering horses ran down across the brook, — all this held us and gave us back our childhood.

Doubtless botanists revel in the flora of the region, for to us laymen the general effect has no less charm, though we are unable to name all the varieties that decorate the scene.

Various narrow and sometimes modern roads meander across the Cape here and there and to us they are fully more attractive than the main thoroughfare. It is here, too, that we find the gnarled pines surrounded by carpets of needles and graced by innumerable little cones. Such an one on a private by-road is shown whose artistry is enhanced by a cling-ing vine.

THE BAYS AND SHORES OF THE CAPE

WELLFLEET has its estuary which at full tide, bordered as it is with waving sea grasses, is most appealing. Farther out through the town we come upon a hostelry, built on a dock. Americans are not nowadays, at least, a sea-faring people, nor do they love the sea, nor do they love the water like the British people. We have noted here and there inland, or on the seashore, boathouses and every preparation for water journeys, but many an instance we know where from year to year the boathouse is not opened and many other instances where it is opened but once or twice. The English seem natural water dogs, and they go boating not as a fad, but because they cannot resist the tempta-tion. One can but note how few and far between are the American coast

BLOSSOMS AND GRASSES—ERVING

THE JOHN ALDEN HOUSE—DUXBURY

WELLFLEET ESTUARY

FALMOUTH LILIES

points where boating is much indulged in. Before the days of railroads it was otherwise. Now the entire flavor of the shore life is being lost so far as playing or laboring with watercraft is concerned. Even at the bathing beaches it has become a joke that the fair bather spends her time upon the sands and seldom wets her feet. The delight of battling with the water seems to have been lost out of the American temperament, with here and there an exception which proves the statement.

The harbor at Wellfleet is one of the few of considerable extent on Cape Cod and at one time the district was a center for whalers. Provincetown appears busier on the water than other Cape regions except possibly one or two of the larger centers near Hyannis and Falmouth.

The artist on the Cape may find much inspiration in the long tongues of shallow water that creep through the lagoons and wind serpent-like in the marshes. About Orleans, on Pleasant Bay, and on the road to Chatham there are wonderful curving shores and tufts of marsh grass and dune reflections that enable one to become lost in the spectacle and linger long in the late afternoon and into the afterglow, heedless of the call of hotel repasts.

As a summer site what can exceed in beauty some high dune looking over the shimmering sea which plays in and out with indefinable contour lines along the sands? Here and there appear a winding bit of road, a clump of hardy pines, a cluster of poplars. Above there is today a flock of the sheep of the sky feeding on the azure plains, tomorrow a curdled mass of wide flung clouds, and the next day the glories of purple, gold, sea-green and the entire gamut of the rainbow list. Rising, spreading, changing until the chameleon-like clouds assume not only in color but in form a variety of aspect which must seem to a savage race as, indeed, it should to us, the play of God with nature!

To those who love change, Cape Cod is infinite in her variety! From summer to summer her coast line changes. One season she fills up an estuary and opens another far away. Some say that in time there will be no Cape. Others would say that once the Cape ran far, far out to sea beyond its present bounds and reached its long finger toward fabled Atlantis. The Cape stands for the beauty and instability of the earth.

Continuous dredging, far beyond the commercial warrant for it, would be required to keep deep water at some small ports where once the arctic whalers rode at ease.

Thoreau describes the Cape in a storm. The usual traveler sees it only when it is on its good behavior, — when it is putting its best foot, or perhaps we ought to say its crooked finger forward. Then it can be most alluring. It is the Calypso of the Massachusetts coast, charming us on to admire her softer and playful moods and leaving us totally unsuspicious of the fierceness of her wrath, when facing a boreal blast she waves her ruffled train of sand and howls with the furies of the storm.

Cape Cod is now an island. There are drives each side of the canal for its entire length and both are pleasing.

SUMMERING ON THE CAPE

SAD to say, the Cape is becoming fashionable. The Great War increased the importance of Chatham as a naval station and all the region of the south shore westward from Chatham is now being possessed, so far as hotel life is concerned, by Society, with a very large " S." If this trend continues there will inevitably follow the construction of many large, modern hotels. At present it is almost impossible to secure accommodations except one provides far in advance. Sophistication possesses all the south shore and although here and there many pleasing summer places, some modest, some pretentious, escape the whirligig and vapidity of the centers, one finds too much of transported but not transformed metropolitan life. The shops are branches of the well known city caterers to luxury.

We ourselves, who are given to the collection of antique furniture and its allied subjects, find no lack of places where the wise and the foolish

A HAZY WOODLAND—ORLEANS

NANTUCKET CHARM

WHERE CHILDREN PLAY—NEAR HYANNIS

THE THATCHER COTTAGE—YARMOUTHPORT

congregate seeking some old heirloom. It is true that one sees perhaps a chair which leaves him puzzled. It reminds him of the professor in entomology whose students thought "to put one over on the old man." They took the body of one bug, the thorax of another, the head of a third, the wings of a fourth and fifth, the antennae of a sixth and the legs of a seventh and further decorated the nondescript creature with such odds and ends of insect creation as pleased their antic fancy. After carefully connecting these incongruous parts into the semblance of a strange creation they took their bug to the professor and stood about in a body while they said, "Will you please tell us the name of this bug?" "Gentlemen," he answered, after a sardonic glance through his glasses, "I will. It is a humbug."

In looking at this chair those who really know will recognize a pair of front legs that have known each other long but are unacquainted with the legs behind. The rungs are recent neighbors who formerly were far apart. The stretcher "knows no brother." The slats are certainly wondrous between such posts and the seat is a marvel of oddness. The offerer of this striking piece of furniture, who possibly himself is merely passing it along from the genius who contrived it, will, indeed, give you its name called after some of the great masters of old cabinet work. Nevertheless, my friend, remember what kind of a bug it is!

We are not saying that the dealers in these wares are anything like as unethical as the farmer who, also by the roadside, displays his baskets of fruit, always with the fairest on top. This is something which no dealer in antiques would do. Nor do we intend to hint that the dealer in heirlooms misrepresents one half as much as the average advertisement of a city emporium. But what would the Cape Codder do in summer without a resort to such a shop where he may sharpen his wits against the Parthian, the Mede and the Elamite? And if the deponent saith true he is against an efficient grindstone. Not for a moment, however, would we be understood to intimate that the purchase of such articles is any more dangerous or deceptive than a flirtation with a girl of doll-blue eyes, nor more dan-generous than a speculation in real estate next door to this same shop, nor more dangerous than motoring on a summer Saturday. Life is so full of its perils and just now it is fuller than usual. All we do wish to say as to the aforesaid dealer, is that he is every whit as good and as bad as his neighbor; that he is not a bit different from folks; and that he has an advantage merely in this, that the buyer is more ignorant of a good chair than of a good potato or a good house lot, and therefore is at a disadvantage.

Perhaps the largest summer industry of the Cape is the disposal of Victorian antiques, which are very real and honest, as pre-Revolutionary relics. Some of these " came over " and some of them " come it over " us. They probably were not on the first lading of the Mayflower, but please remember she has lately been found to have made various other voyages and who knows what she brought! But with all the strictures that have preceded this sentence we gladly allow that the west end of the Cape has lately brought to light two of the most marvelous pieces of the Seventeenth Century furniture known to antiquarians. It is the spirit that moves the prospector for gold that is also found in the seeker for old treasures on Cape Cod. Mankind are by nature, and often by training, gamblers. They love the thousand to one chance and if they would all stand up to be counted how few of us there are who have not taken that desperate venture! It would be well worth while to spend a summer to run to earth one treasure that the Cape gave up a year ago. The finder lost his chance by being a trifle too canny and to the writer was thus opened his opportunity. Others labored and he entered into their labors.

Another industry of the Cape which may be said to have added to its picturesqueness, but perhaps not to its calm and beauty, is the innumerable wooden whirligig toys that ride their wires and poles by the wayside, painted in colors such as no sunset ever showed. It is little to be wondered at that the windmill figures largely in these toys because it is so scarce on the Cape. In fact, we think there is scarcely a region where windmills are more rare. A few, indeed, of these fine relics

A PROTECTING HOME TREE—FRAMINGHAM

MORNING DUTIES—NANTUCKET

WHITTIER'S HOME, NEAR AMESBURY

QUINSIGAMOND BIRCHES

A VILLAGE MANSION

abide, and some have been incorporated into homes, and others are tea houses or show places. The march of improvement and the tooth of decay have alike contributed to their extinction.

To the average citizen an attractive summer on the Cape is perhaps to be obtained most easily by the purchase or lease of a Cape Cod cottage from which little journeys may be made as one lists. If the Cape continues to grow in popularity it is likely to stand out as the most distinctive of our American summer resorts. It is even a question of whether it may not surpass Newport. Happily, fashionable folk no longer look to the exquisite hills of Berkshire County with the same undivided attention as formerly. The trend to Cape Cod is no less than a furor, and when all its advantages are considered one can hardly say that it is too much sought. Ridiculous experiences in stuffy kitchen bedrooms or low and torrid chambers, or even in barns, are now met by the unwary traveler, not forewarned of the great demand for accommodations.

If Cape Cod is to sink into the sea and be forgotten, obviously Americans intend to have a good look at it first.

It is an old axiom forgotten every day that we find what we are looking for. If we look for gimcracks, gimcracks will be produced. If we want beauty we shall find it, or if we look only at the surface we shall not see below the surface. Those who come to Massachusetts with the discerning eye will be filled with the sense of the pathos in her past and will respond to the meaning of her efforts, whether or not those efforts have reached full accomplishment. The spirits and the true hearts of all ages thrill to the same chords and answer to the same beckonings. The deep without speaks to the deep within. Whether it is a picture or an ideal it means whatever the largeness of our nature can grasp. History is " bunk " according to the apostle of the mechanical age, but those who are making history naturally carry on faithfully all the great beginnings which the ages have left us. To them Cape Cod is not a sand bank but an adequate foundation where truth and honor and an outstretching faith limned forth in the sky a permanent and glorious state in which human character was to reach a dignity transcending time and space and capable of making every square foot of the earth prophetic of perfection.

IN AND ABOUT PLYMOUTH

THERE is no spot on earth more significant in human history than Plymouth. There is less to speak of the past here in the way of adequate recognition in worthy monuments than one would hope for. As a child the writer wandered through a stone-cutting yard on a Maine river and looked up to a huge stone forearm which loomed high above him. Many years after he saw the massive granite monument at Plymouth of a female figure, we can scarcely say feminine, where that same hand points upward. It is the colossal misfortune of America that she desires monuments but largely lacks the artistic genius. Had the execution of the Plymouth monument been equal to its conception the result would have given us a proud shrine for the peoples of the

BELOW THE DAM—FRAMINGHAM

HONEYMOON STROLL—WESTMINSTER

PROVINCETOWN   NAN OF NANTUCKET

broad nation to visit. Yet the motive was good. That generation tried. It had the ideal but it could not embody it in stone. The monument stands for love and faith and truth, indeed, but the expression of these qualities is somewhat short of what it should be.

The Standish monument at Duxbury is a graceful shaft, but Miles was far away from us on the summit and the lightning recently cast him down. If we catch the meaning of his character at all, he was a man never up in the air but had both feet firmly on the ground.

We have to think of Duxbury and Kingston and the adjacent regions as Plymouth for once they were so. They belonged to the colony as an historical and spiritual entity.

We have, indeed, in Plymouth a very satisfactory statue of Massasoit, evidently a man of much native nobility whose fine physique and character have been cunningly apprehended by the sculptor.

At Pilgrim Hall, now made a permanent structure, there are certain priceless memorials of the Pilgrim days, but there is nowhere in Plymouth nor, for that matter, in America, a worthy house of the Seventeenth Century restored and furnished as the second Pilgrim generation would have had it. No museum has a full representation of the household economy of the Pilgrims. Such an assemblage was very easy to secure ten years ago and is not wholly out of the question at present. But there has not been in any one man or corporation at once the knowledge, the zeal and the resources to attain this very highly desirable accomplishment. Further, the real American, aware of the general lines of the Mayflower, must have blushed at the nondescript affair which came into the harbor of Plymouth during the great recent celebration. We know the contour of the Mayflower and we know its dimensions and it is entirely feasible to re-construct such a vessel of old timbers and place it in a ship house. Such a work, set near a dwelling in which all parts should be strictly accurate historically, would be more interesting, more educational and a finer work of patriotism than anything ever done in America along these lines. As this is written a photograph comes to hand of an apparently correct Mayflower just constructed in California by descendants of her passengers.

The persons appointed by the national government to pass on improvements in Plymouth were not specially fitted either by taste or education for their duties. Their sojourn in Plymouth was very brief. The state of New York has spent great sums in the purchase and reclamation of Seventeenth Century houses, but the state of Massachusetts which has greater reason for doing that thing has never done so.

We may rejoice that the water front of Plymouth was very satisfactorily improved and that the Rock has been placed under a dignified canopy. The bold bluff above it, however, should be in the possession of a patriotic corporation or of the nation itself.

There are one or two dwellings in Plymouth which have in them material from Seventeenth Century structures or possibly were erected themselves in the latter part of that period, but for the most part the growth of the town has obliterated such ancient landmarks. The most dignified and worthy and interesting feature of Plymouth at present is Pilgrim Hall and its contents. Here one may go repeatedly with delight and profit. Referring to what we have said elsewhere regarding Cape Cod wrecks, the ancient skeleton of a vessel, exhumed from the Cape Cod sands, now in the basement of Pilgrim Hall, fills one with a sense of our nearness to that period, and with astonishment at the small size of the craft that dared the Atlantic and sometimes, as in this case, dared fatally.

The gardens of Plymouth, bits of which we show, are among its more pleasing features as we call to mind the English custom of having a flower plot in front of every cottage.

The most striking feature about the township of Plymouth taken at large, is the great number of fresh water lakes, one being named from the black sheep of the Mayflower, "Billington Sea." These lakes are increasingly valuable as water supplies. The region south of Plymouth is a striking example of the scrub growth of oak and pine which is so

FRAGRANT WAY — MOHAWK TRAIL

THE ROAD TO UNCLE JONATHAN'S — BERKSHIRES

TYRINGHAM WATERS

SLENDER BIRCHES—STOCKBRIDGE

common in this part of the state. We find Bradford in his history lamenting the continuous exodus from Plymouth and its slow growth after more than a generation had elapsed since the settlement. Such a condition was inevitable, since better lands called to a people engaged almost exclusively in agriculture, excepting only fisheries.

The Major Bradford house in Kingston on the road to Duxbury at Jones River has lately been redeemed. If one stands well back from it on the front it affords a very good example of the second period of Colonial houses. It may be hoped that in the process of time greater knowledge and resources may endow some of these early houses with valuable contents matching their period.

It is markedly true not only of Plymouth but of most other Massachusetts towns which have grown beyond the small village stage that they have lost most of their simple and quiet architecture. No doubt this is inevitable. It is not set down here as an adverse criticism but only to call attention to the fact that if we would see a village as it was a hundred or a hundred and fifty years ago we must go to one which has not developed into a mart or into a manufacturing center. In this particular, Kingston, Duxbury, and Marshfield have an advantage over other towns more nationally known. They retain many of the early edifices, and although the Seventeenth Century house is uncommon, something more than one hundred such houses have been tallied, and perhaps two or three hundred between York, Maine, and New York City and up the main rivers of most ancient settlement.

The occupants of early houses are themselves frequently lacking a special study of early architecture and as a consequence, having lost the authentic records of changes made in their dwellings, if any such records existed, these residents are not seldom mistaken as to the date of their dwellings, but they are more frequently mistaken as to the date of the present appearance of these dwellings. Very few of these early houses have escaped what were thought to be improvements. The same remark may apply to furniture. We have often observed owners far more taken up with furniture of their Aunt Sarah than with that which preceded it by two or three generations and was ten times as important from the historical and constructional point of view. It is practically impossible to find a house of harmonious style throughout, still less such a house with interior decorations also in keeping with its time.

The first range of towns inland from Plymouth was also on an inferior soil, and it is not until we get into the vicinity of Taunton and towns of about that distance from the shore that we see marks of general and successful cultivation of profitable fields.

The two main routes from Boston to Plymouth are both most interesting and quite different. Some of the villages like Cohasset, Scituate and Hingham possess numerous fascinating old dwellings and one can consume weeks in a thoroughly satisfactory meandering over the main and cross roads of this entire section.

A comparison is often made between the better lands and the greater development of the north shore to the detriment of the south shore. This distinction is not warranted so far as regards that part of the south shore within twenty miles, we will say, of Boston. Not only are there many fine fields, but the development of this region is certainly more attractive than that on the north shore south of Salem.

AROUND AND ABOUT BOSTON

THE Fenway drives of Boston present many fine stretches, chiefly beautiful for the meandering lines of the water-ways. These are all together on the south side of the city. Boston approached from the west also escapes unpleasant driving features, as one enters at once into the better part of the city. To approach Boston from the north with any degree of agreeableness one must swing around through Cambridge and, even so, there is much that one could spare. From the northwest the approach is rather agreeable along Massachusetts Avenue.

MIDSUMMER GLORY—STOCKBRIDGE

BALCH HOUSE, BEVERLY, BEFORE RESTORATION

ELIZABETH IN HER GARDEN — FRAMINGHAM

THE WINSLOW HOUSE, MARSHFIELD

There are large marshlands to the north and northwest of Boston and it is probable that they will never be redeemed to beauty as there are so many obstacles. At Medford, however, and in Cambridge tidal dams and systematic dredging have obliterated the mud flats and the formerly offensive conditions at low tide, and have made the Charles and the Mystic real sources of beauty rather than of ugliness. This is a highly satisfactory piece of work and redounds to the everlasting honor of those who toiled for it so long and so faithfully.

The Charles, itself, between Boston and Cambridge has also been redeemed by filling and holding it to its course, and the bridge work so far undertaken and that which has been projected is of such a character as to give the city a distinctive and noble setting as viewed from Cambridge. In fact, we do not know of an American city that can compete with Boston in these respects.

New York is frankly constructed of pyramids of masonry and the writer is so averse to such Babel structures that the work of an etcher like Pennell cannot lure him to believe in their beauty.

Within Boston very little remains of the earliest days. The Paul Revere House has been rescued but such was its condition and such is its setting that it loses much of the nameless charm afforded by mellowed age and freedom from encroaching modern edifices. The Old North and the Old South churches and the Park Street church, eloquent each of various periods of teeming history, are with us yet. But these and the various other structures, old and new, which go to make up the notable architectural features of the city are so well known on picture cards that we have here paid them little attention. The State House is, in its way, a true center, all humor apart, of American history at its best. Opposite its entrance is what is properly regarded as a most distinguished sculptural delineation, the uplifting and satisfying Shaw Memorial.

The tower of the Perkins Institute and the more recent tower of Boston College, each noble and well set, afford an atmosphere of strength and beauty redolent of the finest traditions of Europe. It is not in vain and not without reason that Boston is felt to be in America the radiating point of the better earlier aspects of art, of literature and of human liberty. While the low aims and wilful lack of knowledge of the multitude are ever seeking, and often with success, to dominate in Boston as in all the other great cities of the world in all periods of history, we should not lose heart. There is an undying spirit of beauty. Eternity is hidden in the heart of man. Touched by nobler forces, men awake out of the low levels of selfishness and prove themselves capable of high desert from their country. The triumphs of the bruiser in municipal government by shaming the great mass of well-meaning men, finally shame himself. Out of crudity and brutality have arisen in the past the finer effects of civilization called out by the spirit of evolution which we are just discerning is no other than the spirit of God.

Much that is alien seethes in modern American life but perhaps there is in it a vitality and drive lost out from the old stock. Let every man be estimated at what he is and not in reference to his ancestry. This is not the first age of the world to manifest the fact that those who dwell most in the deeds of their ancestors often show least that is commendable in their own.

A MAY DRIVE—WELLESLEY

THE BRYANT MAPLES—CUMMINGTON

NANTUCKET DOCKS

PILGRIM AND PURITAN ICONOCLASTS

IT has so long been a habit of conceited, modern Americans to think of our ancestors as stern and hating beauty, that they have fairly persuaded themselves and most unread persons that their viewpoint is correct.

In the history of the town of Sudbury there is a quotation from the town meeting records well back toward the middle of the Seventeenth Century wherein " it is also ordered that the backside of the meeting house be made hansom." We have here the instance of the average man of the Pilgrim generation giving his judgment that beauty belonged in his life and that it was appropriate in the edifice where he worshiped. We have no reason to suppose that this instance is unusual. We have every reason to believe that it was the rule rather than the exception.

Interest and ignorance have reasoned that image breaking meant lack of appreciation of beauty. It would startle some who so think could they see a piece of furniture owned by Cromwell as exquisite in all its lines, as dainty, as delicate in its fancy as one could hope to find in any age. And we now, who have in our generation lambasted our ancestors for their lack of artistic appreciation, are going back and copying with the most faithful care the edifices which they erected because we have no modern styles, good or bad, and we are obliged to hark back to the Pilgrim century for the best inspiration in art and architecture. The most important pieces of American Seventeenth Century furniture are eloquent of the Renaissance. They are, indeed, degraded from its finest features. That beginning of degradation is a part of the inscrutable decline of taste which culminated not only in America but in Europe in the nineteenth century.

There were religious reasons which seemed sufficiently cogent in the seventeenth century for hating statuary, especially if it had any suggestion of ecclesiasticism connected with it. We do, however, find maintained a reminiscence of the Gothic in the domestic architecture of that day, and a degree of taste in carrying out home decoration that may shame our recent generations.

The character of the Pilgrim fathers, at least, was mild and kindly, as anyone who reads what is left us by Bradford and Winslow must conclude. The distorted religious views exemplified by Cotton Mather in pushing on the prosecution of witches was not in any respect peculiar to him or to America. One has only to run lightly through English history of the same period to find that amid all classes, prelatical and ultra-protestant, there was a universal superstition against witchcraft. The fact that this persecution was localized in America goes far to prove the greater breadth and sweeter humanity of the immigrant as compared with the dweller in the old world.

One would think, to read the partial and distorted references of many of the " humanists " in the nineteenth century, that witchcraft persecution arose out of the " orthodoxy " of the Pilgrim generation. This dark aspect of history had no more to do with the reformed faith than with the moon's phases. People of every creed and no creed at all took up the hue and cry against witches. Many did it from conviction, many from the universal tendency of the mob to side with leaders, but mostly they did it because they were the children of their age and took for granted what is abhorrent to us.

Religious conviction is always respectable even when it is horrible. Thus viewed, the people engaged in that persecution were white saints in comparison with the wholly diabolic Herrin mob, by which more perished than in all our witchcraft craze. Every age has its special sins and our age is certainly second to none in this regard.

The settlers of Massachusetts were simple men, no more brilliant than those they left behind them in England. They did, however, rise to a better embodiment of the Christian spirit at Plymouth than was commonly found in that day. The sound common sense of the people of Holland with whom their leaders had dwelt influenced them. The Pilgrims have also suffered from the bitterly unjust saying of Holmes

A SUNBURST BED—QUINCY HOMESTEAD

BLOSSOMING WAYSIDE—FRAMINGHAM

THE GOOSE CHASE QUILT—QUINCY HOMESTEAD

A BACK COUNTRY BROOK—WORCESTER COUNTY

about their falling first on their knees and then on the aborigines. His spirit should have been too large, and as the writer believes, was too large, to have uttered this libel seriously. Nevertheless, as in the famous case of Doctor Osler, he was taken seriously.

There perhaps has never in human history been a case of more notable forbearance and patience in dwelling with a savage people than was manifested by the Pilgrims toward the Indians. The march of Winslow through the forest and his unselfish treatment of Massasoit when that chief was rescued by him from an otherwise fatal illness is a chapter in heroism and an exhibition of human nobility such as is seldom found on the pages of history. It was the swashbuckler, deep-drinking colony of Merrymount that brought on the notable instance of trouble with the Indians. Superficial writers would have us believe that the pure simplicity of the life of the Pilgrims made them especially bloodthirsty. Had it not been for Morton and his ribald crew the fierce and terrible flash of Miles Standish's wrath would have been unnecessary. Standish, by his alert boldness, saved the colony. It was the desire, the prayer and the practice of the Pilgrims for a great many years to live in utmost peace with their neighbors. Perhaps no colony settling under similar circumstances has ever been more free from violence. These are the simple facts and a decent regard for truth compels their reiteration.

THE NORTH SHORE

THIS district is preëminently the fashionable shore resort of America not excepting Mount Desert or Newport. It is fully as accessible from the South and West as is Newport and far more accessible than Mount Desert, whose beauties and incomparable excellencies are a thing apart, reserved only for those who seek the best irrespective of its location.

Before one leaves Lynn he has a fine experience passing over the natural causeway to Nahant.   This is an imporatant side trip if one loves the sea.   Several of our pictures are on the bold shores of Nahant, so long the residence of Senator Lodge.

The wonderful drive along the north shore beginning from the vicinity of Lynn and continuing into New Hampshire and indeed into Maine, is a joy of a very distinguished sort awaiting those who have never passed over it.   The great improvements of late years have supplied a safe road and stalwart bulwarks against the sea.   The beaches have been redeemed from shoddy features.   Dwellings of high character have sprung up in the more fashionable districts.   The country just back of the waterfront which has been given the name of Middlesex Fells is an amazing mass of boulders.   The improved Newburyport Turnpike which passes through a portion of this district, though uniquely straight right and left, is far from a straight line up and down.   Hence its monotony is broken by fine sightly crests over which it marches.

The traveler going directly to Newburyport misses the fine features which render Cape Ann a locality perhaps not second in interest to any in the country.

As Salem is the point of divergence for this journey and also is itself a town unique, we glance at it first.   Its great fire did not destroy much of its ancient architecture.   Its delightful old streets are still redolent of the early eighteenth century.   It is true the Witch House is disfigured by the wart of a modern shop added to its front.   The proprietors are possibly unable otherwise to retain the edifice but it had almost as well be obliterated as to be in its present form.   In the autobiography of Joseph H. Choate the house is shown as it was in the earlier part of the nineteenth century.   It is also shown in other aspects in the January 1923 number of " Old Time New England."   One may hope that a dwelling so flavored by a vital and characteristic though awful period of history may sometime be restored to its early condition.   The supposedly first brick house of the town, at last accounts was still neglected.   The highest praise is due to Miss Emmerton for her efforts, so largely successful,

THE STREAM—MOHAWK TRAIL

THE SEVEN BRIDGE ROAD—LANCASTER

A FALMOUTH WATERSIDE

THE DINING ROOM—QUINCY HOMESTEAD

THE CRADDOCK MANSION, MEDFORD

in restoring the House of the Seven Gables for the romantic and literary tourist. She has also done distinguished work in connection with other dwellings.

Lately also the more recent but quite typical Nichols-Pierce mansion has come into the hands of the Essex Institute, at whose headquarters so much that is important in early American history is preserved.

All in all, Salem is perhaps the finest center to study the old town life of America with the possible exception of Portsmouth, New Hampshire. Salem, being older than Boston and happily not so large, has been able to retain much of its earlier flavor.

Just before reaching Salem one is called off by the lure of Marblehead. Wonderful old houses remain here, there being at least three or four of great distinction which are all available for examination. Perhaps the Lee mansion has a parlor as interesting as any in the North, or, if its prestige is challenged, that can be only by the parlor of the house in Danvers, perhaps not open to the public, which was built as a summer place by " King " Hooper.

The bay of Marblehead is a gem of beauty and one who loves at once natural scenery and old America finds them both in this town at their best.   One is here away from the bustle of the city, yet by no means distant from the attractive features of American outdoor life. Marblehead is a yachting center; its harbor gay with snowy winged craft; its streets uneven, winding, full of surprises, and its back country appealing from its variety of roadsides.

We lightly pass over most of those features which properly belong in the guide books and holding to our quest for natural beauty chiefly, go on our way.

Through Beverly to Manchester and Gloucester the semi-urban condition prevails.   Here and there in quaint nooks one may ferret out an early and picturesque dwelling.   Largely, however, the commonplace or the grand modern house predominates.

Gloucester, the north shore center for deep sea fishing, impresses the sensitive traveler with the tragedy of that calling.   The fact that men are still found to undertake fisheries off the Banks is one more instance to prove that humanity follows its bent, irrespective of the dangers along the way.   An occasional salt like " Fishin' Jimmy " may still be found about the littoral, overhauling his nets.   Gloucester is divided between its fishing for cod and for tourists, and more and more it is succeeding in the latter quest.   The splendid bold shores about Bass Rock and Magnolia where, whenever the floods lift up their waves, the eternal conflict is resumed between cliff and sea, give the wanderer the sense of unlimited powers still at work and allow him to take up into his wearied person the strength of the sea.

Rockport, the last land on Cape Ann, is also the last mainland resort to compete for marine conditions in summer similar to those on Cape Cod.   Rockport is a smaller and less sophisticated Gloucester.

Following the Newburyport Turnpike from Boston one finds at Lynnfield that curious institution in America — a district lying back from the town that gave it its name and was originally portioned out by the people

HONEYMOON WINDINGS—WESTMINSTER

PIERCE-LITTLE PORCH—OLD NEWBURY

ABERJONA WATERS—WINCHESTER

UP THE LANE—NORTH ANDOVER

of such a town for farm lands. This is more like the continental scheme whereby people leave their village dwellings and spend their days on their more or less remote lands. Just back of Lynn, Salem and probably other towns there were areas owned by city dwellers who were perhaps engaged in other activities than farming but who, nevertheless, depended in part on farm lands to which they went in summer or from which they drew their supplies. At Danvers there is a notable instance to which we have referred in the " King " Hooper house, a wonderful mansion erected as a summer home by the merchant of Marblehead who was so successful and so ready to expend his substance in a lordly way that he got his epithet. In Danvers, also, there are fine outlooks and in the valleys remarkable old dwellings which we have pictured and others which are perhaps worthy of closer attention, as the Rebecca Nourse House, the Danvers Historical Society House and various others which invite a pause.

Much that is interesting is found on the cross roads leading off the Pike; for curiously the Pike itself has no villages of any considerable size upon it. At Topsfield village is a unique house, that of Parson Capen, having the gable and front overhang, a combination probably not well matched elsewhere in America. Approaching Newburyport, some of the Dummer Academy edifices fascinate us.

In Newburyport itself there are perhaps more three-story houses of the period of 1780 to 1800 than in any other similar area. The stately High street and many other streets are filled with such houses. While the style of architecture is not of the best period, the dwellings were, nevertheless, built with the greatest care and the hallways are very attractive, many having the divided stair which turns both ways from the landing. This town and many others in Massachusetts have historical societies housed in quaint dwellings affording no end of interest.

As one goes north from Salem through Beverly and Ipswich to Newburyport there are innumerable calls to the eye in the ancient homes. The Ipswich Historical Society which has its headquarters in the Whipple

House, sometimes called the Saltonstall House, near the station, has what is perhaps the most remarkable room in America. We refer to the great fire room with its cross summer beam and its wonderful paneled gunstock posts supporting the cross summer. Whoever wishes to see the earliest American life at its best should examine these great beams and posts and get the fine effect of solidity which they afford.

At old Newbury the Pierce-Nichols House, off the road, supplies us with a marvellous porch which is not equalled elsewhere in this country. Its beginning in stone and terminating in brick, its niche over the door for a lantern, sundial or saint as you may choose to decide; its thick wall, quaint windows and tile floor give a suggestion of Old England in New England. The heavy walls, the deep window embrasures of the stone house show an English effect and the remarkable buttressed chimney built in part on the exterior of the rear, is only rivalled by the stone house of Guilford, Connecticut. The dwelling we describe is not shown except by the courtesy of the owners. It is set amid broad acres of the original great domain and for a manor house in New England presents more features true to the ancient life than we shall find elsewhere.

On the main road is the remarkable dwelling now used as an inn, belonging to the Society for the Preservation of New England Antiquities; the Short house on the opposite side, and not a few others have very early and rare features. And so we come again into Newburyport by this second route. On the river here is what, in its day, attracted much attention, being the first suspension bridge in the region. The drives by the river, mostly cross roads, introduce us to alluring glimpses. Going from Newburyport through West Newbury to Haverhill one passes a great many very early houses and mounts the crest of lofty ridges and crosses fine water reaches, so that all together this drive may be commended as among the best in the country.

PATCHWORK QUILTING—NEWBURYPORT

A HYANNIS COTTAGE

TEA IN THE STATE CHAMBER—LEE MANSION

THE HOPE OF THE YEAR—HARVARD

THE RARITY OF GENIUS

A TRAVELER in England is very much struck, as he goes from one provincial town to another, at the absence in the guide book of great names which stand for national glory. In a newer country like ours we find this scarcity still more marked. How many towns of five or ten or even twenty-five thousand inhabitants one may pass through that are not notable for any personality of genius! Even the mechanical genius in which this country is so rich, can by no means be found in every part of it. There is, to be sure, a notably high average quality of citizenship such that a great many persons in each community exceed the knowledge of the ancients in some departments of human thought. Where all are distinguished, none are distinguished. With all these allowances, however, one feels jealous of human reputation when any particular neighborhood fails to shine in human annals. Someone has said that only one life in a hundred millions is remembered permanently. The estimate is large. A poet has commemorated the fact that we have evidence of the existence of some great nations of which not a name remains. " They had no poet and so they died."

This little essay would inquire why genius or, if you choose, great distinction in a certain line of human effort, is so rare. The probable answer, it would appear, is not the obvious answer, namely, that supreme talents are rare. Genius has been defined as the capacity for hard work. Is not the answer in this, that so few men of excellent ability have devoted themselves by choice deliberately and intensely with all their faculties to the accomplishment of an outstanding achievement? This is not to say that any well-educated man of good ability can be an Emerson. There are fine, inherent qualities which, added to intense application, have placed certain names on the roll of geniuses. What we contend for is this, that men like Poe and Burns, had they not dissipated their powers, might have left us great epics rather than brief fragments. Even Lowell, it is thought and as he himself has hinted, might, had he set himself steadily to the task, have left us a literary monument far more superb than the work he has left. Here we would hazard the judgment that probably no town of ten thousand inhabitants has failed of men who, had they set themselves to one fixed purpose of creation, would have left a permanent monument of achievement.

When we stand in the midst of some fair landscape and see the brilliant play of light and the glory of earth and sky, and the wealth of teeming nature, we are conscious of a sad regret that so much fair preparation, that so fine a theater for action should have failed in the production of great men. England is broad, but has only one Runnymede. America owns a single Concord. Massachusetts can pride herself that so many foci of power are located within her narrow limits. But with the preparation of an education in liberty and law and the call of a new world, we at times wonder that no more has been done after such great beginnings. Somebody, some years ago, worked out the probable number of living descendants of the Massachusetts Coast Colonies at fifteen millions.

The names in "Who's Who" have recently been classified by states and it has been found that the quota for the eastern states and, particularly, for Massachusetts, is far larger in proportion to the population than in the newer states. Yet we must believe that indolence is responsible that many men of fine abilities stop short of the highest achievements. The Yankee character has been supposed to be restless. The descendants of the first settlers of Massachusetts should frankly admit that there are multitudes of them in the back wash of civilization. We have in mind a fine scholar of large native powers whose broadest influence did not extend beyond the occasional office of a selectman in a town of six hundred people. There are always ten times more persons who will die for their country than will live for it.

The superficial have accepted as a final dictum the ancient saying that "in making many books there is no end." We make no pretensions

CONCORD BIRCHES

GOING BACK TO NATURE — WORCESTER COUNTY

NEIGHBORHOOD GOSSIP—SAUGUS

DREAM AND REALITY—GRAFTON

A NANTUCKET THREE DECKER

to wide research but we think we voice the experience of many when we say that scarcely a week elapses that we do not seek and seek in vain for authoritative information in some department of human knowledge. To an astonishing extent, history is blank. The notorious phrase of Napoleon that " history is a legend agreed upon," while a trifle too broad like all proverbs, is so far true that we blush. Scientific information is still at a premium, and, far beyond necessity, literature is lean.

The world war is scarcely over, yet many of the greatest movements in the war are veiled in mystery and probably always will be. What we do know in comparison with what we easily might know will always be an infinitesimal fraction. Here then we plead that the youth of Massachusetts, with the background of their history and the standpoint of their present opportunity, may dedicate themselves in sufficient numbers to the accomplishment of important work that never has been done.

NEW ENGLAND IN WINTER

THE recent increase in interest in out-of-doors winter sports is awakening many persons for the first time to one of the aspects of beauty which ought long since to have been a larger factor in our thought. The curling snow fingers that fall gradually away in curves from the old picket fences; the white festoons that drape the evergreens; the old door posts with their caps of snow; the graceful birches laden with their white burden and drooping in bows of every degree of curvature until some even meet the ground; the half-hidden cottages; the fantastic aspects of the snow shapes in their draperies and wave effects, — all these are charming elements of northern winter life.

The snow itself has recently been found to be a mine of hidden beauties hitherto neglected. An enthusiast who has made three thousand individual magnified photographs of snowflakes has so far found no two alike. If a mathematician were called upon to compute on the theory of chances the probable number of regular crystalline snowflake forms he would give us an answer high up in the billions. Most of these forms are hexagonal crystals. A very great many of them may supply exquisite patterns for embroidery, for lace and for every sort of designing. Little do we think as we set our foot on the first snow that we are probably crushing a million crystals each of great beauty, each individually distinguished. One of old made the query, " Hast thou entered into the treasures of the snow? " Did he suspect this modern revelation? Probably not. The stars under foot are as wonderful as those overhead.

What a delicate inconceivably subtle influence must guide formations of these crystals so that each follows a new design! We are led to wonder whether there is a limit to these designs.

Snow in certain forms, crystallized under very low temperatures, sometimes produces a three-sided crystal. These are not so beautiful but they are, nevertheless, extremely interesting.

The snow in the open is influenced in its contour wholly, of course,

ECHO LAKE — BERKSHIRES

FROM BERKSHIRE HEIGHTS

THREE FRIENDS — FRAMINGHAM

in the same way as water and sand. A duplication of a curdled sky may be seen in many a snow landscape and again on the blowing sands which are here and there to be found in New England. The shape of a sea wave is often duplicated to a nicety in snowdrifts which curl at their crests with all the delicacy possible. The spindrift of the sea is also duplicated in the loose snows which blow from the crests of such drifts.

We are greatly indebted to the recent fashion of wintering in the country because it is possible the fashion may awaken dwellers in the country of rigorous winters to the desirability of their place of residence and to its winter charm, scarcely inferior to that of summer. The mass of mankind, largely untouched by intrinsic beauty, may be led to see beauty, when it becomes a fad to do so, and, all unconsciously to themselves, persons may awake to recognize the splendors which have hitherto lain, asking attention, around them. It is beyond our purpose if it is not beyond our powers to describe intimately many phases of winter beauty. These themes have furnished the poets with no small part of their inspirations. The recent work of Mr. Daniel L. Cady in describing the homely occupations of the country has filled a void in our literature which was in great need of treatment. Under the guise of dialectic forms and from the mouth of the more or less untutored farmer he has expressed many shades of rural life in a manner which shows the keenest observation. The importance of such work is understood by those who know how rapidly the old rural conditions are passing away. There are many things which are already almost archaic in American life, and to preserve a pictorial and literary record of them will very much assist us in securing the rotundity of history.

UNCLE HY'S COLT

THE beautiful snow is availed of by the farmers for breaking colts. Uncle Hy was a burly man of heroic build and when he heard of a colt that had grown to a complete horse estate without ever having admitted a master he thought he saw his opportunity, as the price was not too much and the animal was a beauty. A sturdy horse sled that could not harm itself whichever side up it dragged, and afforded easy means of getting off, was the chosen vehicle.

Now, this colt like some other beauties, was proud. His neck was clothed with thunder and he sniffed the battle from afar. Yet, externally there were no emphatic marks of wilfulness. We will not call the colt obstinate, we will say he just had plenty of character. You have seen such — horses, possibly mules. This colt was not dull. It is said that horses with brains can be taught. This colt knew too much. His mind worked rapidly, but not in the same direction or at the same moment with Uncle Hy's mind. The colt would go rapidly and stand sturdily; only when Uncle Hy said " Whoa " the colt went along, and when Uncle Hy said " Giddap " the colt stood still. It was a failure in the meeting of minds. Consistency may be the mark of a bigot. This colt was not consistent. He could change his mind as rapidly as a woman. If one could only have foreseen when he would change it and in what direction it would have simplified life for Uncle Hy.

When Uncle Hy was not saying a word, man and horse would go along together quite smoothly for a moment or two, when of a sudden the colt would determine to go across lots, which he did, over walls, fences, gutters, stumps and obstacles, all and sundry. The depth of the snow somewhat eased the bumps only they came at unlooked for moments when one could not see what was beneath. Anyhow, Uncle Hy held on. He did not say a word; partly he lacked the breath, and partly it was his nature that the madder he got the less he said. He would come in after a half an hour or half a day's bout with his colt,

ACROSS THE FARM—ENFIELD

A MARLBORO ROADSIDE

PLYMOUTH

NANTUCKET

rather haggard and weary for a man so strong. His arms had been pulled half out of their sockets and his clothing bore no marks of recent acquaintance with the tailor. In fact, he had been in the trenches, and he came away with things not originally on his garments, although parts of them had been left behind in the experience. No doubt the colt was strong; so was Uncle Hy. But Uncle Hy was not scientific and the colt was. Asked why the colt did not keep the road, Uncle Hy would not admit pigheadedness on the part of the horse, but answered, " I guess he jes' tuk a notion."

Uncle Hy had never heard of skis nor did I ever know him to wear snowshoes. He required neither, so long as he fellowshiped with this colt. There was exercise a-plenty, and fresh air moving past at an alarming rate and an intimate acquaintance with snow banks. It was winter sport of a strenuous and absorbing character.

In the dim distance we cannot now recollect how long the association continued, but we do remember that it was finally dissolved by mutual consent with pleasure on both sides of the partnership. Before the end came, however, much history was written and many places were visited " where man never trod before." The neighbors helped, or they tried to. Fifield thought Uncle Hy whipped the colt too much. Uncle Laban thought a colt should be touched up with a whip. Cottle was of the opinion that the animal would go along all right if he was let alone, but Uncle Hy wanted to go with him. Young said Uncle should talk pleasantly to the horse, Uncle was saying nothing eloquently. No one could say the colt did not try, only Uncle Hy seemed not to speak his language.

What was desired was synchronism between the front and the hind legs. Instead they worked like the escapement of a Simon Willard banjo clock. Sometimes when Uncle Hy suggested that the colt go along the animal went into the air at the forward end; sometimes when it was desired to stop him the rear end went up. There was nothing the matter with either end, but the harmony which Uncle Hy sought seemed lacking. The colt was a self-made horse, satisfied with the job. That he could acquire a high school education all by himself was a mark of genius. Most horses can go ahead or back up. In addition to these movements of progression and retrogression the colt could move sidewise to shame any crab and follow any given diagonal provided you did not give it to him. Furthermore, the animal had humor. At one moment he was all fours in the air, body uppermost, and again he was rolling in the snow all fours in the air. He loved the snow and it was a joy to him just to be alive. There was no doubt the animal was a philosophical entity or some parts would have come loose in the experience of that winter.

Coming in from a playful morning with the thermometer well below zero both man and horse were in spots in profuse perspiration, which showed good blood and proved that they had not lost a moment. Uncle Hy had frost on his eyebrows but fire in his eyes. The colt was like Borah. You never knew what he would do next, but you knew he would do something and do it without consulting anyone. His purposes were subtle and his mind serene. He had the infinite variety of Cleopatra and like her was fitted to entertain any man.

CHARMING MASSACHUSETTS VILLAGES

PERHAPS Williamstown is the most attractive village in the state if we consider its surroundings, its college atmosphere with beautiful edifices and its general attractions. While among the hills it is not low except as related to the mountains. One looks up from it, indeed, to the loftiest peak of Massachusetts, Greylock. When one leaves North Adams and swings north toward Pownal, Vermont, the view of the valley is one of the most superb in our experience. Not so much has been said of this as of the Deerfield valley but perhaps it is because that valley is an historic region.

A LEAF STREWN BROOK—UXBRIDGE

THE WAY THRO' THE ORCHARD—GRAFTON

AUTUMN KNOLL—CHARLES RIVER

Williamstown is just near enough to North Adams, a considerable center, to be agreeable and accessible; near to the Hudson, to Vermont and to the valley of the Berkshires lying to the south, and it is on the Mohawk trail. It is a region of delight from which one can easily depart toward every point of the compass. The grouping of the college edifices which dominate the village is well done. Asked what was the most desirable residential village in Massachusetts the author replied, " Williamstown."

We find it is true that in every town there is something meritorious that no other town has and Massachusetts is so rich in beautiful old villages that the last one we are in is always the best.

Greenfield is a peculiarly delightful center. Though in the Connecticut valley it is not immediately on that river but on the Deerfield. It has, of late, taken on more importance and there is no more charming location for a small market town. It is on the main motor routes north, south, east and west and has the power of holding tourists.

Northfield for quiet and simplicity and moral tone is probably not surpassed. It lacks the magnificence of country places in the Berkshires, has a less rugged setting and is very accessible. Yet its very lack of mountains near at hand makes its scenery somewhat less striking and one contents one's self there with the features of rural life and with the religious atmosphere. It is a town ever memorable as a monument to one of the greatest and best of men, Dwight L. Moody. It wins many people who do not care for the luxurious entertainment of more fashionable resorts, but love the plainness and democracy of a New England village of the earlier time.

Deerfield is really a suburb of Greenfield although its people would perhaps prefer not to have the matter put in that way. Deerfield is the most famous small village so far as old houses is concerned.

Pittsfield has outgrown the village stage. It is, of course, the central point in the Berkshires, being on the Jacob's Ladder trail and on the main Berkshire route north and south.

Whether this region is always to be fashionable or not, the visitor who judges a country by what it is, must ever grant, and that with gladness, the remarkably winning features of this great county.

The run over to Lebanon is through a region of rolling hills with fine outlooks. The routes south to the finest residential sections of the Berkshires appeal to every lover of a fair landscape. To the east Dalton is a trim high village; and Hinsdale, higher still, lies in a fine setting of hills.

The birches of the Berkshires vie with the elms. A little south of Pittsfield there is a wonderfully fine avenue of these trees on a little field road by the river. Their massive size is a surprise to all not reared in the New England hills.

Lenox might have been, before it became so thoroughly taken up with fine country seats, a rural village of surpassing attraction. Even now one loves its situation, but men have done so much here that their work often calls our eyes away from nature.

Stockbridge still has a village atmosphere that is thoroughly good. Many of its summer guests have entered into the life of the town in such a way as to benefit rather than to kill the local spirit. As the seat of a very early mission to the Indians and as the home of Jonathan Edwards, the town, looked down upon from Monument Mountain, is the very acme of an old New England center at its best. The marvelous elms of the main street are still mostly in good condition. One who skirts the golf course here will perhaps obtain finer compositions than in any other similar range that we know.

While Echo Lake has its charm and Stockbridge Bowl its own beauty we would say that the river followed through the town affords more contours of loveliness than any other water border. Stockbridge as the home of one of our greatest sculptors and as forever fragrant with the memory of Joseph Choate, men who brought down the traditions of an earlier culture and a fine character, is a town which, when its history and its inhabitants, its setting, its present welcoming and attractive features are considered, certainly has a strong pull upon the author.

THE GREAT HINGHAM ELM

GLOUCESTER HARBOR

DEDHAM

KING HOOPER HOUSE—DANVERS

FASHIONABLE 'SCONSET

Lenox, Stockbridge and Lee are often considered together as a social unit. Their lines run into each other so harmoniously and the nature of the summer places is so generally similar that one thinks of the district as a single neighborhood. It is the western outlet of the Jacob's Ladder route, lately greatly improved. Tyringham is a side valley as yet out of the stream of fashion but deserving as much attention as its better known neighbors.

Lee is rich in admirable river views. The orcharding of all this region is being carried on with active competition for the favors of the local fairs and in blossom time all the lower slopes are a mass of delicate color.

Great Barrington, the southernmost of the better known Berkshire communities, being at a considerable distance from Stockbridge, has a separate demand on our attention. The drives through the Egremonts

present views of very extensive nature, and if one loves great elevations
certainly it is on the slopes of Egremont that he would quite naturally
make his home.

The mountain towns surrounding those Berkshire villages which we
have mentioned invite us to excursions where the simpler country life
continues. Some of the roads are not as wide but most of them are
negotiable. The southwestern corner of Massachusetts is a region of
extensive highlands so far not taken up by city residents as generally
as the valleys. There is a calm and aloofness of physical atmosphere,
a sense of being at the top of the world, in these neighborhoods. We
cannot and would not deny that the little house on the hill is a more
powerful magnet to us than the great house in the valley.

New Marlboro on the other side of the Housatonic and the little
seen remoter districts east of it will probably in the course of time afford
summer homes for the great mass of Americans who need an opportunity to think and an air to breathe neither of which is available in the
summer in our great cities.

Sheffield is a small and somewhat less sought yet attractive valley
town. Berkshire county, being large and extending from Vermont to
Connecticut and bordered by New York on the west, is strategically
located to catch the eye of most Americans. It contains many small
villages whose names even would make a large index, but almost all of
them with certain features that single them out in our minds with pleasing recollection. In one there is a fine old spire; in another dignified
early houses; in another little cottages of alluring coziness; in another
a little landscape of exquisite contour; in another some historic name has
left its aroma. In all of them there is health, a considerable elevation
above the sea, a population of character and culture. Many of these
villages are now being made accessible for the first time by improved
roads. A little lake as entrancing as old world waters of which poets
have sung; or a winding way about a hill crest opening a miniature
empire of fertility below; a wood with the fine trunks of primeval trees

PUTTING IN ANCHOR ROPE—GLOUCESTER

A LITTLE MAID OF FALMOUTH

standing in their silence and dignity through the generations, — all these call us on from turn to turn until we profanely wish for more lives that we might spend one in each of these little centers of delight.

How far the Berkshires will develop and in what direction is one of the questions that this generation must try to answer. The ideal society is not to be had in a region exclusively given up to great estates, neither is it to be had in a region where small hill farms and meager provision for education are altogether predominant. There is an opportunity and a hope that the Berkshires may develop along the lines of the best English rural communities having their more beautiful estates owned by people who love to be gracious and have a powerful sense of their obligation to the community; to make it a real center of strength in the best elements of American character.

We may hope that the owners of the fine estates will at least be so assured of their positions through their personal merits that they will not be afraid to mingle with our humbler brethren lest their distinction be obliterated. Always the noblest and wisest are the simplest. Always whoever holds himself aloof obviously fears that he cannot bear comparison with the average man. If a person cannot establish his preeminence by his inherent worth, his insight, his sympathy, his native ability, then he deserves no preëminence and ought not to desire it. To be loved is the most important thing in life and comes before the possession of a fine place in the country.

The gentleman of the perfect simplicity which marks a distinguished sculptor never cares for his position in the world, because he holds it by too secure a tenure to fear the touch of common men.

One can understand the objection of owners of great estates to having a gaping crowd running over their grounds and peeking in at their windows. Their country homes are for quiet and not for caravans of the uncouth. And, happily, in this fair region, it is not necessary and not even desirable to enter private grounds to see horizon outlines that thrill one with their material splendors, to take in wide valleys fair with placid reaches of river reflections. No one can wall in nature. The open road is pure socialism so far as it goes and it goes far. A disposition is quite noticeable in some sections of the Berkshires on the part of the summer resident to give the best of himself, which is his heart, to the neighborhood in which he dwells. A country that is good enough to live in is a country good enough to diffuse our interest over. We are, if we are rotund beings, present with all our faculties at every spot we visit. We cannot, and we dare not if we could, leave graciousness and culture and ability behind us. To do so or to attempt to do so would be an evidence either that we wore these marks merely as a veneer and were lapsing to a baser manhood or that we thought the best things in character should be confined to a few. If there is good in any man, if there is power, if there is brilliance, he holds these things to diffuse over or to work through his neighborhood and the man who is not good at home is good nowhere. He will not be good in Heaven, and he will not be good when he travels, and he will not be good in his office.

It is a fallacious assumption that we do not carry our characters with us and that we can be one thing in one place and another thing in another place. Mark Hopkins, Emerson, Bryant and all others who had something for humanity diffused it where they were, all the time, just as a rose is as fragrant in one hand as in another. Unfortunately there is a class of persons who try to edge into society lacking that which is valued by society and who, therefore, become bitter and inclined to misrepresent. For our part, we have generally found distinguished people worthy of the positions they occupy. From this category we would exclude those who are distinguished for wealth alone. Even wealth in the hands of a man who has little else is scattered often in beneficent directions. The new rich man must get something for his money and he must needs have advisers. That he so often expends in beneficent public works his gains, however obtained, is a matter for congratulation. The second generation may attain to all those features of the aristocracy of mind and heart which make the aristocracy of wealth bearable. If they

THE PASTURE IN THE DELL—WARE

AFTERNOON IN NANTUCKET—SIASCONSET

fail of their opportunity they are, after all, the principal losers, for there is no man so pitiable as he who, with wealth, lacks taste and heart. He is in the world but not of it, having failed to absorb its finer beauties and to enter into its nobler achievements. He is a shining mark but not worth the powder, because he meets a punishment here and now that is the worst of all punishments. In a world splendid with opportunity he makes no essential place for himself. In a world groaning with travail he fails to enjoy the thrill of coöperation.

There is a vast deal of literature wasted, from Thackeray downward, by the attack of empty heads and full pockets. Given a generation or two the situation is reversed or at least equalized. It is often forgotten that there is a hatred and an unreason amongst people of small means thoroughly pernicious and blighting. For every man, whatever his material condition, there is a vast storehouse of beauty, of moral appeal, of historic and prophetic knowledge, to overflow his mind and soul.

Socrates would not be miserable beside a Dives. Enmity of wealth is the mark of a mind which itself could never deserve wealth.

The Berkshires are a fine arena in which to work out the blending of all sorts and conditions of men in a rural atmosphere. Such a blending is possible to the mutual benefit of all conditions concerned. Such a blending has here and there occurred bringing mutual respect and benefit to all. To those poor in spirit there has come an association with men who have shown by their power in dealing in large concerns, and with their generalizing faculty and their sense of broad issues, a great benefit. To the city denizen and the possessor of broad income there has come the viewpoint of the fine soul that dares not neglect culture for business; that loves fellowship more than directorates; that would rather be neighborly than be a lord of lands. It must have been recognized at least by some captains of industry that there are those who have gained what they have lost; who have deliberately chosen scholarship or art or science as a more delightful and possibly more profitable human occupation than the accumulation of dollars.

The villager who has delved into the motives of men and scanned the movements of history and adapted himself to the needs of his community and contributed by his hand or his thought some permanent good to leave behind him is a sane and serene person without envy or malice. There are Lincolns who never dwelt in the White House to whom humanity means as much and in whom pity is as great as in that martyred President. There are in most rural communities men of heart and soul, of appreciation for the best things of the world, of capacity for giving and receiving, such that their lives are flooded with the wealth of all that is worth while.

ON THE CONNECTICUT

SOUTH HADLEY, the seat of the college for girls, and Hadley, the supposed original home of the Hadley chest, are quaint towns which arrest us. There is also Hatfield, on the other side of the river, from which wonderful old door heads have been carried away. The writer found one house being used as a tobacco barn on which there was a marvelously fine door head, the pilasters being running vines with fruit and flowers. The owner had built what he thought was a fine modern house in front of the old dwelling and had torn out the old interior. Another house in the same town had the walls of its parlor divided into panels by bands of stiles and rails carved with vines. They were all torn off and burned up to modernize it. Oh, Fashion, what crimes are committed in thy name!

Longmeadow has what so many towns lack, a feeling of the connection between the name and the place. A stretch of narrow waste land extends for the most part for many miles up and down the eastern bank of the Connecticut and one would well keep in the main north and south track. The Longmeadow street divided with a broad park strip between the two drives and graced by numerous elms and flanked by excellent houses is a sight long to be remembered. There is more of this town that is good in a straight-away direction than one will find in a long search.

PETALS IN THE PATH—LANCASTER

HAPPY VALLEY—FRANKLIN COUNTY

THE WAY TO SOUTHBORO

NEWTON MEADOWS

DELIGHTFUL EXCURSIONS FROM BOSTON

THE guide books are excellent for historic sites but cannot attend particularly to selecting beautiful landscapes. We, therefore, submit a list of various drives which are attractive for nearly all their extent and which lead one past various beauty spots of Massachusetts.

1. Proceeding out Commonwealth Avenue and crossing the Charles River, in less than half a mile you reach a fork where the main road to Weston swings right. Ignoring that fork, keep straight on, swerving neither to the right or left through a fine wood and Cochituate village. Immediately after passing its four corners you reach the causeway over Cochituate Lake, an unexcelled spot for lunching under the beautiful pines. This short causeway is a revelation of beauty on a quiet day and a most desirable resting place. A pine grove affords a parking ground, and the silence and seclusion are perfect.

Running on from this point and swerving only where necessary and making no short turns you enter Framingham Center, whose old common is one of the best in this country, having no obnoxious features in its circuit and without the intrusion of shops or ruinous buildings. The old town house at one end and the church at the other; the fine colonial school on the one side and the great stone or wooden colonial residences on the other, distinguish it. After circling the common one may resume his journey via Pleasant Street to Southboro, which is perhaps the most English town in America. This entire district between Framingham and Southboro and borders of some other towns is the site of the Metropolitan water works reservoirs. One gets fascinating water glimpses, and the margins of these lakes, partly natural and partly artificial, being neatly kept, give a somewhat but not too emphatic park-like appearance to the country.

On the way to Southboro another causeway is crossed and one sees at Southboro a charming village group of buildings and also a waterway connecting two lakes. The slopes toward this waterway are thoroughly

English in their gentle, well-kept surfaces, and the residences are of a fine or unobjectionable order.

One must pass well through the town straight away to get this glimpse. One may then keep on to Northboro or swing back through Southboro to Marlboro and there take up the Wayside Inn route to Boston. The Inn, a few miles east of Marlboro, is, in its setting of oak trees, perhaps not equaled elsewhere. Agassiz used to say that these oaks were from twelve to fifteen hundred years of age. The old highway formerly ran directly by the Inn door, and it has been, happily, swung out now to one side. We may express the hope that the Inn may be preserved in its quainter features. The gambrel roof is considered one of the best type and has been much copied. An ancient print shows the house without this roof and we know that gambrel roofs were very rare before 1730, only one instance of such a roof being known. It is probable, therefore, that if the Inn was erected in 1700 it did not have a gambrel roof orginally but that this roof is the effect of the first improvement, which in this case we can only commend. The route thence into Boston for some miles is marred by many roadside advertising features, but grows better in South Sudbury and Wayland, both charming towns, and in Weston particularly one finds a district of marvelous beauty. We refer to the good handling of the landscape features as a setting for homes and public buildings.

One can wander all about from Weston to Kendall Green and back by various roads, or to the south, taking one road and returning by another, and can scarcely make a mistake. The most attractive route into Boston from Weston is to the right over the bridge of the Charles by which we came out. An alternate route is directly back through Waltham, Watertown and Cambridge, passing Mount Auburn and following the parkways in Cambridge by the redeemed Charles to Massachusetts Avenue Bridge.

2. We may leave Boston by the same bridge on Massachusetts Avenue and keep this avenue through Harvard Square, pausing for the exam-

THE BEAUTY OF THE UPLANDS—FRANKLIN COUNTY

GREAT WAYSIDE OAK — SUDBURY

THE COMING OUT OF ROSA

ination of many notable old edifices in connection with the university, and passing on through North Cambridge, Arlington, Lexington to Concord. There are several houses of much importance to examine in and about Lexington and the village green there is not only superlatively interesting to patriots but it is as beautiful as it is sacred. The town has recently bought and to some degree restored the Buckman Tavern, an instance of very fine public spirit as the cost was great.

The old road to Concord is the more interesting. Concord may hold the visitor for many hours with its bridge, its monuments, its inns, its quaint and historic homesteads, its literary shrines and Sleepy Hollow cemetery. Here is a village reminding one very much of towns in the English fen country so far as landscape is concerned. The Concord river in its meanderings over the meadows of the town is very seductive. One should circle all about the village on various roads for some distance in all directions, because in returning, perfect landscapes appear with the village in the distance. It is a place of waters. It is a notable fact that this district seems healthful. One hears of little malaria, and the sages of Concord lived to a ripe old age. There is scarcely an uninteresting mile in a considerable circuit around Concord. Lincoln is a town abounding in soft curves of road or stream, fine clusters of elms and evergreens and stately old homesteads.

One may return to Boston by digression to Bedford, where the Stearns house on the left is a beautiful example of its period, and thence one may go back to the Hub through Lexington. If one cares to extend this route, although it is ample as laid out for a day, one may go on from Concord to Acton, Littleton, Ayer and Lunenburg, thence through Pepperell to Tyngsboro and down the Merrimac to Billerica, Burlington to Boston, keeping the through tour route and leaving Lowell on the left. Or, shortening it a little one may make a turn at Littleton Common or Chelmsford and thence back to Boston.

3. A northerly drive is through Cambridge and Medford intersecting the Paul Revere route, and northerly through Stoneham and Reading to

Andover and North Andover to Haverhill. There is no finer hill town than Andover with its unrivaled assemblage of academic buildings. The Academy has now taken over the old seminary buildings and added them to those formerly belonging to the academy, and it is equipped in a manner that would startle our English friends who think we have little in this country architecturally. Of course, one misses the dominant ancient Gothic effect, but there are a great number of competently erected edifices in excellent taste. Running to North Andover and Bradford, one passes many of the early and now highly improved country homes, some with their seventeenth century panelled chimneys. The landscape is fair and sweet and broad-reaching to the eye in every direction.

Entering Haverhill one may go on to Groveland and West Newbury on the way to Newburyport. On this leg of the journey there are water reaches, and noble outlooks, and seventeenth century houses following one another in a rapid and irresistible succession, appear, so that one never knows which is better, the hill, the valley or the homestead. But one does know that each is many fold more attractive in combination with the others. We have previously referred somewhat to Newburyport and the routes thence to Boston.

4. Taking the Dedham road from Boston one may there diverge through Needham and Wellesley to Framingham, passing many windings of the Charles. From Framingham we return through Sherborn, Medfield, Walpole to Dedham and may follow the Fenway into the city, going by the western avenues and returning by the eastern drives of that extensively beautiful district.

5. From Boston through Massachusetts Avenue to Mattapan, Ponkapoag, Stoughton, South Easton to Taunton is a straight and not always very interesting route, but there are elements of great beauty here and there. From Taunton to Middleboro and thence back through the Bridgewaters to Randolph and Brockton to Boston is a feasible return.

6. There is a way to Plymouth by which after one reaches Quincy one may not double on his track extensively, from Quincy by the inside route

A BIRCH MEDLEY—BERKSHIRES

A LAST LOOK—QUINCY HOMESTEAD

A SOUTHERN BERKSHIRE ROAD

QUICK WATER—HAMPSHIRE COUNTY

through Accord and Hanover to Kingston.   On this route there begins
to appear quaint cottage life of the earliest settlers.   One returns via
Duxbury, Marshfield, Scituate and Cohasset.   The Jerusalem Drive from
Cohasset into Quincy, where one meets the outgoing route, is justly famed
for its loveliness of cove and rock and island.

These suggestions by no means exhaust the principal ways of beauty
that diverge from Boston, but they include the most important thoroughfares.

7.   It is almost always safe in the touring season to diverge on any
Massachusetts by-road, in the eastern portion of the state at least.   We
do not enter here upon a full discussion of the Providence road.   There
are fine digressions from this as from Wrentham, Franklin, Bellingham,
Milford and Grafton to Worcester or from Wrentham to Foxboro, Norton
and Taunton.   The route from Providence shortly takes one into Massachusetts, going into Seekonk and Swansey to Fall River, one of the most
beautiful drives imaginable.   Or one may go directly from Providence
to Taunton over a road affording very satisfactory scenery of old houses
and orchards.   One may return from Taunton to Fall River or return
to New Bedford, Mattapoisett, Wareham, back through Middleboro to
Boston.   It is better having made the journey from Boston, we will
say as far as Middleboro or Plymouth, to make New Bedford a second
center of touring.   There are so many inlets and little taverns and lovely
water reaches that one is too hurried if it is desired to return to the great
city before night.   New Bedford is wonderfully alluring as a touring
headquarters.   Its museum, called the Dartmouth Historical Society, has
many features not found elsewhere.   Its various shops where quaint
things are sold, its water sides and its environs may hold one for days,
and there are more agreeable accommodations in the way of lodging than
formerly.

8.   Tours about Worcester: Following southerly from Worcester
through Oxford to Putnam, Connecticut, one comes, near Webster, upon
the lake with the long name, Chauggoggagogmanchauggagogchabuna-

gungamaug. What this word means is said to be a thousand bays, but we do not guarantee the correctness of the etymology. It means to some people a stutter if not worse, but it is easy if you know how.

Returning to East Village east of Webster one may pass to Douglas, East Douglas, Sutton and Millbury back to Worcester, but this return route is not a main thoroughfare and one must be prepared for concentrating his enjoyment on the streams and ponds and back country in general.

The main route from Worcester to Providence passes through Grafton, Northbridge and Uxbridge, following the line of the Blackstone river, which, while said to be the American stream most thickly studded with manufacturing towns is, in spite of that, often beautiful. Arriving at Worcester, if one does not care to keep on farther, one may cross over to Bellingham and thence back to Worcester by Milford, Upton and Grafton. The east and west route from Worcester is the main Boston and New York thoroughfare. We have covered this route going west from Boston as far as Marlboro.

The slopes from Worcester into Shrewsbury open up fair prospects and thence down to Northboro there is much of interest. This road, however, is swarmed with vehicles and is more like a trunk line railway than a quiet touring journey. Westward from Worcester by the same main line one finds at Leicester a high and attractive village. One is now in the highlands of Worcester county, the backbone of the central part of the state. It is a general elevation of the whole territory. There are broad and smooth fields stretching away to a great distance. At East Brookfield one may diverge to North Brookfield, a very pleasant journey, and a little west of West Brookfield one may turn north to Ware and its charming river valley, coming back to the main road at Palmer. The route from West Brookfield through Warren to Palmer is essentially a region of little mountains, each side of the Quaboag river, a stream which offers us many a shimmering reach of placid mirror and many a rapid of herring-bone water.

BUCKLAND

THE SHOCKED CORN—MILLIS

The hill crest and cloud effects through this region are not enough enjoyed, as people on this main road are always going somewhere about as fast as they can. But when the mists flirt with the hill crests, now touching, now withdrawing, and when the sunlit slopes change from green to brown to pink and to purple in the westering light, one should pause and consider that this heavenly vision is for him.

A farmstead nestled on a high slope and looking out over the splendors of the valleys and the hills and the changeful sky supplies a joy always present when man nestles in the bosom of nature and thoroughly adapts himself to his surroundings. These hills are as gorgeous as the Berkshires and are no less beautiful. In fact, some vistas which open on this drive are, when we review them in memory, a most sweet reminiscence.

From Palmer one may strike back through Brimfield to Southbridge and thence through Charlton to Worcester. This route is over the higher hills and at Brimfield one finds a little rural village that appeals to the imagination. Also from Brimfield opens a new southerly route into Connecticut which when completed will be a more popular way than that now usually followed through Springfield, because it is far from the beaten track and one does not, all the way from Southbridge, coming from Worcester, or Palmer, whichever the point of departure, pass through, until he comes to Hartford, anything larger than a rural village.

There is another short journey of interest from Palmer to the Monsons, though it is better, perhaps, to return at the end of the good road, or one gets into a country too rough for motoring.

Westward from Palmer to North Wilbraham, if one diverges to Wilbraham and thence to Springfield, the road is not so jostled and the old town of Wilbraham is attractive not only from its fine trees and roadsides but from its academic traditions.

We have indicated return journeys to Worcester from which we should take still another journey. For instance, going back through Palmer by the main route will furnish a very good day's excursion.

Going out again from Worcester to the north to West Boylston we come upon the great Wachusett reservoir. We believe this is the largest lake in Massachusetts. If one chooses to skirt the lake from West Boylston to Clinton, down through Boylston Center back to the starting point, he will see a variety of landscape, all, as it were, made by man, since the lake contours and the water reflections have entirely changed the scenery.

As one leaves Clinton one should pause to go out on the great dam, the noble and massive work of engineers, which did not forget to be beautiful.

If one chooses to keep on from West Boylston north through Sterling to Leominster and Fitchburg he will find a pleasurable journey. He may then go from Fitchburg to Athol and thence back through Barre to Worcester. But this Worcester-Athol route deserves very much more attention from the lover of beauty. Beginning from the Worcester end two stretches are open, one through Paxton and the other through Holden, the two roads meeting at West Rutland. That through Paxton has a fine stretch of woodland. That through Holden and Rutland is very high and sightly.

Through Colebrook Springs to Barre there are small water glimpses of unusual beauty, and at the foot of Barre Hill is one of the best of that kind. A wood road of perfect beauty is part of this journey. From Barre into Athol is a road probably second to none in the exhilaration of its long high stretches over the highlands. Petersham is a summer resort and an old-fashioned village located on the back-bone of the state. The soft, long, sweeping slopes from each side and the far-reaching views give one something the same impression as on the journey through Palestine north and south.

There remains to us one more excursion, at least, from Worcester which should not be omitted: that to Wachusett Mountain by Holden and Princeton. Shortly beyond Princeton Center as one enters the mountain road the fair prospect of the state eastward to Boston and the sea seems to show one a map in relief of a vast territory. To our thought the region around Wachusett is destined sometime to be more highly

WELLESLEY WITCH WATER   NANTUCKET GOSSIP

A GLOUCESTER PETER

A PEEP AT THE HILLS—CHARLEMONT

appreciated.   It is the nearest mountain peak in Massachusetts to the great centers of population, and is, therefore, the only spot inland for many miles around, where one can be certain of mild summer air.   Many cross roads from this region, while given no attention on touring maps, are yet attractive.   One can approach Princeton from the east through Marlboro, Hudson, Bolton and Lancaster.   Between Sterling and Hubbardston, going directly through Princeton, one finds in the laurel blossom season hillsides which are solidly covered with its flowers.   Before leaving Worcester one ought to have a day or two about Lancaster, which we believe to be the town containing more great trees of many varieties than we have elsewhere seen.   An oak, a buttonwood, about as large as any, a maple, an ash, and an elm of surpassing diameters were all there until lately, when the Queen Elm went down in a storm.   The tree was thought to be the largest elm known in our country.   Many years ago we placed a horse and cart behind the tree to hide them when picturing it.   The rear of one wheel tire and the tip of the horse's nose were all that were visible, although the animal and vehicle were arranged not endwise but crosswise to our vision.   This tree had a circumference exceeding twenty-six feet at one's shoulder, and of it Holmes wrote:

> " Where the broad elm, sole empress of the plain,
> Whose circling shadow speaks a century's reign,
> Wreathes in the clouds her regal diadem,
> A forest, waving on a single stem."

It is said, by the way, that Holmes used to carry a string in his pocket and slyly measure the elms in England, and that he felt some chagrin to find that they slightly exceeded the noblest he knew in America.   He might easily, but for poetic limitations, have extended the century to three, which is about the probable life of the largest old specimens.   The forest effect which he so finely brings out may often be observed by the springing of a half dozen branches almost celery like, and giving the impression of a woodland in themselves.

In some pasture also we find a maple with an almost perfect demidome top and a foliage at the base about seven feet from the ground. This curious formation on the lower foliage of trees in pasture lands arises no doubt from the browsing of the cattle. It is seen in California to perfection on the sharp slopes where grow the live oaks whose branches will parallel the hillsides downward and upward almost precisely.

In North Lancaster the Seven Bridge Road is a wonder of elm foliage. The trees are self planted and at places grow like a gigantic hedge and at another point opening sufficiently to permit the development of massive columns. The Thayer family were pioneers in Lancaster in beautifying the landscape in a broad way, and the region for miles around is an exquisite example of country life in America at its best.

These remarks include Harvard, whose orchard ridges are marvelous in their beauty, so much so as almost to be unique. Bolton may be included in this same orchard neighborhood and Sterling as well.

There are considerable regions in Massachusetts which, according to the common phrase of the farmer, are fit only to hold the world together. It would be gratuitous to point out such districts, but we wish to puncture the cockiness of the westerner who thinks slightly of our Massachusetts farms. The writer has journeyed in every state of the Union, and lived in two western states, several years in each. He has yet, however, to see any fairer farming tracts than many in Worcester county. The same remarks might be made of districts in Essex, Hampshire and Franklin counties. There is an abundance of scrub oak and thin gravelly soil here and there in the rough back country of the state. In such regions the dwellings become ruinous and the number of inhabitants consistently shows losses in the census. These so-called abandoned districts are much talked about east and west. The fact is they are of small importance considered in a broad way. Their total number of inhabitants is small, and if their churches are abandoned it is because there is no one to attend them. It is obviously absurd to consider running state roads through all such districts. The land is gradually being abandoned to the encroachments of forests. This is as it should be. It is a natural water shed and wood

THE WAYSIDE INN APPROACH

A DEDHAM BANK

A NEWTON OCTOBER

OLD CHESTNUT STREET—SALEM

A GAMBREL CORNER

reserve country.   A state utterly fertile everywhere could not afford woodlands.

9. Springfield, Holyoke or Northampton may be chosen, as one's tastes suggest, as a center for exploring the Connecticut valley.   From Northampton to Holyoke, to South Hadley Falls, South Hadley, the Notch to Amherst and back to Northampton by way of Hadley includes a range of

meadow and hill so agreeable that one could not regret the tour. Amherst is in a fair open plain. The river cutting the Mount Holyoke range affords the only contrast in the region between mountain and stream.

The outlooks from Mount Tom or Mount Holyoke are of an unusual character in America, resembling more the Hudson highlands than most of our viewpoints, because of the river below. Such views as these are not to be seen in the White Mountains. There we have the continuous ranges of other mountains, here the broad and fertile valley of the Connecticut not surpassed for fertility nor, in its specialties of culture, by any region, are spread below one as well as the tortuous windings of the river.

The journey through Northampton through Williamsburg and the William Cullen Bryant region of Cummington to East Windsor, thence to Dalton and Pittsfield, is one of the newer mountain thoroughfares which were discovered to Americans and now available for their convenient inspection, districts capable of providing a rest region for the future of teeming America.

There are one or two offshoots from the Jacob's Ladder route as one goes west from Springfield, the great and in many ways delightful city of western Massachusetts. The route to Westfield is through a plains country, but at Woronoko we reach the windings of the hill roads. There are digressions here. There is another one from Huntington to the north through a region of wonderful possibilities and present splendors of hill and valley. At Chester one may climb again to the north from a main road over the heights.

Springfield is sufficiently far from Boston to have a thoroughly individual development. Its public buildings vie with those of Hartford. One may possibly question the appropriateness of the Italian architecture in New England, but its beauty considered by itself cannot be challenged. Springfield often considers itself, we presume, much as Los Angeles in California, as the natural center of its state. There is a virility and an enterprise and an intellectual development, such that the city has claimed and been accorded for generations to be the sufficient source of all urban

A CAMP—QUINSIGAMOND

A MANCHESTER BIRCH DRIVE

THE DOCKS—GLOUCESTER

THE TIN PEDDLER

influence, that is needed for many miles around. It has taken on, late years, the character of a metropolitan center. The total population near or tributory to it has risen to pretentious numbers. By its strategic location and its alert and energetic leadership it has started on its career like some great western cities to claim national prominence. The province of our book does not permit us to dwell extensively on urban matters but we must at least pause to rejoice in the vigorous life and prophetic future of Springfield.

THE OPEN FIRE

MANY persons still know by happy experience the soothing, dreamy effect of an open fire.

Our word " hearth " goes back to the roots of our language. Even persons of very active temperament can gaze at the witching blaze of an open fire and be content. Its play of color and fantastic shapes, its spitfire and its glowing embers are invitations to dream. Back of this, of course, lies the completest chain of heredity known to human beings. The oldest of all sentiments has grown at the hearth into human consciousness. Warmth and protection, a sense of home, the memories of every progression of age in a single human life and in all life are all gathered into the mystic web of unconscious memory. From the hearth came the savory dish after a day of fierce battling with wild beasts and wilder elements. The earliest waking knowledge and dawning affection were born at the hearth side. The boy there learned the lore of his tribe. There the family councils were held.

In their old age our fathers sat huddled in the chimney corner, fondling their grandchildren upon their knees.

The hearth was the focus of the house. In its modern significance there is a fine flavor. It was the fountain, the center, the core of life. It was the glowing source whence emanated all humane civilizing currents, and there at last our fathers were gathered to their fathers.

Let us not break that priceless chain but maintain one room at least where a little open fire may call us about it at evening. Thus we shall keep the connection with that vast mysterious stream of hopeful humanity which was and is and is to be. Thus we shall have unity with history and our sympathies will be warmed by this curious, wondrous potentiality, — a human life, born in mystery, existing by struggle, passing into shadows but big with gleams of a far-reaching, wondrous, rising future.

The fireplace is shown in this volume in many of its aspects. We have in the huge early form its rounded back and plastered wall as in the parlor (p. 80). Little recesses were constructed in the rear ends of the fireplace to hold the tinder and keep it very dry. A seat was sometimes actually built into the end so that on chilly days when a bit of fire was needed for the aged they might sit in the chimney corner.

The somewhat later kitchen interior of the Revolutionary days, was a storehouse of every necessary household utensil. Our ancestors did not seek to hide the culinary utensils but displayed them with pride. Their open dressers and walls, hung full of iron spoons, forks, ladles, skimmers and skewers, were almost an education in themselves.

As plenty was secured, our mothers of five generations ago embroidered by the fireplace with their pointed frames capable of being swung as they willed.

In the backs of the fireplaces were great ovens built bee-hive shape as in the Hazen house, Haverhill, always called the Garrison House. It has two such great ovens each swelling into a closet at either side of the fire-place. These ovens had no separate flues but the blaze kindled in them rushed out of the door and up the chimney. When they were well heated they were raked out and the baking was done by the process of absorbing the effects of the previous heating. This was the true fireless cooker. Such an oven would keep warm twenty-four hours and remain hot for twelve.

On bitter days of winter the work was done near the fire. The apple paring and the pie making amused the small child and stirred the sense of domesticity in the sturdy yeoman who came in from his labors.

BLOSSOM LANDING—WILBRAHAM

HUNTERS' ISLAND—COHASSET

SHADOWS ATHWART—LANCASTER

A NORFOLK FARM LANE

The fireplace of the earlier time had an arch above it to serve as a foundation for the hearth in the chamber above (p. 176). In this, the Cooper-Austin House at Cambridge, said to be the oldest dwelling in that city, the pie is being taken from the old oven.

The cat was a happy addition to the fireplace. She gave the last touch of domesticity and was almost as important as the cradle, as a part of the composition (p. 156). This fine old place, the Gates house, near Framingham Center, is nestled under the hugest and most beautiful elm anywhere known. It covers the dwelling, the highway, the lawn, the walls. What a contrast to the characterless numbered dwellings of a city street which have no possible distinction. In an old house like this all the timbers know one another and their owner. He has inspected the stones of their foundation. He has remedied incipient decay. He has protected their roofs against the storm. He recollects the history of the changing generations who have dwelt there. Every room is a monument of a great event. Every chamber knows the going and coming of life. In the parlor weddings have occurred for generations. There is not a nook but is redolent with the comedy and tragedy of life. The old home has made good its place in the world. The generations have gone past in their procession over the highway. The setting of the home, every slope, every path, every gable, every arching curve of branch above, every stone in the wall is part of memory's picture. Life is enriched and ennobled by such a homestead. One cannot say that all generations will be noble born amid such surroundings, but it would be folly to ignore the stimulus to patriotism that such a training must supply. A fine conservative spirit which desires to retain the old homestead and its furniture, although both are marked by honorable scars, is one of the better aspects of civilization.

At a little later time or in the smaller rooms diminutive fireplaces were provided with their interesting mantels where if at all, appeared the decorative tastes of the builders. In such handsome rooms the mistress entertained her friends at " Tea in the State Chamber " (p. 76). In this, the Lee Mansion, Marblehead, we have a very noble example of the taste of the best decorative period. Here, panelled to the ceiling, the parlor is reminiscent of the homes of England. It is past comprehension that a few years ago such places were utterly neglected. It is worth while to recall that this Lee Mansion, standing among the four or five best houses of the North, was sold at auction for $5000, and had not a man of vision in Marblehead happened to drop into the metropolitan office where, far from the dwelling, the property was being sold, it would have been lost to the public. In fact, most of our fine early houses have been thus lost and are now beyond recall. The writer could narrate by the hour similar instances of carelessness and neglect. The King Hooper House at Danvers (p. 96) has been saved to the family which has for a long time held it. Its rooms are also panelled. Aside from the end porch it is nearly as it was, its wonderful rooms a monument of a well-balanced and cultivated coördination of dwelling to inhabitant.

On the fireplaces such as graced the period of 1730 to 1770 in the parlors it was common to use a border of Dutch tiles. The hearth not only in the finer, but in the larger and constantly-used fireplaces was usually composed of brick tile about seven and a half inches square and laid, not as they are now laid with wide seams, but close together. These old tiles are now very much sought. We recall one happy instance where a seeker about to erect a home in an early style purchased a place for removal, the cellar of which he found completely paved with these tiles.

The side and back walls of the fireplaces were always ordinary brick. Pressed brick never appears and in the effort to copy, the use of such brick is clear evidence that the feeling of the old fireplace is not understood. Fire brick were not used on the back, at least not at an early period, and very little anywhere. The continuous disintegrating process of the blaze against the rear brick was overcome by inset fire backs of wrought iron in wonderful old molded forms. Some made at Saugus are still in existence. Such a fire back was discovered in a room in the Winslow house at Marshfield. Sometimes in the earliest period plain sheets of iron were used.

SEDGES AND ELMS—NORFOLK COUNTY

AN OAK-BIRCH ROADSIDE—LENOX

STUDIOUS MAID—ANDOVER

HAZY BIRCHES—BOSTON

Mantels are not found, or found with extreme raity, in the period before wainscoting came in, about 1720. Before that time the chimney tree, as the great stick was called, supporting the bricks over the fireplace, was frankly exposed. This stick was often of oak; frequently of bog oak which would never catch fire. Instances are known of chimney trees twenty inches in depth. The inner side of this great lintel was hewn away on a slope to encourage the smoke to ascend.

Artists of imagination have shown us in mural paintings the beginning of the civilized state symbolized by a fire. The Greek legends regarded fire as stolen from the gods. It is, of course, the first and probably the most powerful stimulus of the human intellect.

At first the fire was built against some cliff shielded at least on one side from the wind. Little by little it was shut in more and more. We think of the chimney as a very ancient institution, but English literature contains notices of the first chimney on the houses of the nobility as curious ducts to carry up the smoke. Before that time the smoke ascended, as among the Indians, through a vent hole in the roof. There are ancient creosoted beams today in many an old English dwelling against which the smoke of early generations rolled. From such beams hams, venison or pork were hung and without any other special attention, smoked meats were obtained.

The writer visited in Alaska the remarkable village where Mr. Duncan gathered the coast Indians and taught them how to live by adopting only those devices of civilization which seemed necessary. His own residence consisted of a main room the center of which contained a square area of sand. Above a tunnel-like canopy, a kind of suspended chimney gathered the smoke and conducted it through the roof. It preserved for us a lively illustration of historical development. Many of the fireplaces in the old world filled the entire end of the dwelling. There is one such in Rhode Island, outside our scope. Thirteen feet is not considered a remarkable spread for a fireplace three or four hundred years old. In that period stone was used chiefly, but it was roughly faced. We cannot enough deplore the thoughtless fad of using round field stones not only for house walls but for fireplaces. No such construction is ever found in good or even simple American dwellings except possibly in the remote and crude Appalachian regions. In some villages people seem to have gone pebble mad, setting up flimsy posts, fences, porches and shaky chimneys of such small boulders. The true fireplace shows an effort at shaping stones for their use and it is this meeting of man and nature, the adaptive and creative instinct, which gives old homes their charm.

The earliest fireplaces have a depth of three feet in some cases and not a few are two and a half feet from front to back. The vast logs were sufficient for the bitterest winter, but as time went on a second and third fireplace of brick is often found constructed within the old one to contract its dimensions and render it easier to supply fuel.

Baking was done not always in the oven, which was a weekly event, but sometimes daily in cast iron Dutch ovens with covers of the same material in which bread was baked "between two fires." That is, the dish was placed upon coals and coals were heaped above it. Rapid action was had and a delicious aroma secured, impossible in modern methods.

The ancient turnspit for roasting was laid on hooks on the andirons. In a well-equipped fireplace there were three series of hooks rising one above another to accommodate the size of the roast and the conditions of the fire. A pulley connected with a minute belt to a weighted jack on the chimney tree completed the outfit, as in the little sketch called " Christmas Expectancy " opening this book.

It was later that the jack supported on a tin rounded screen came in. Such an affair would have been impossible to have used before a great fire. The date of this arrangement was late in the eighteenth century. As the use of the jack was more or less bothersome, boiled dishes were the more ordinary diet, and where a weighted jack was missing it was often necessary to roast the boy while he roasted the meat. So the great pot in which the meat was stirred up by the tormentor, a fork of ominous size, was hung from the lug chains or later on from the crane.

THE NASHUA ASLEEP—LANCASTER

DISAPPEARING IN BLOSSOMS—FRANKLIN COUNTY

A BERKSHIRE POOL

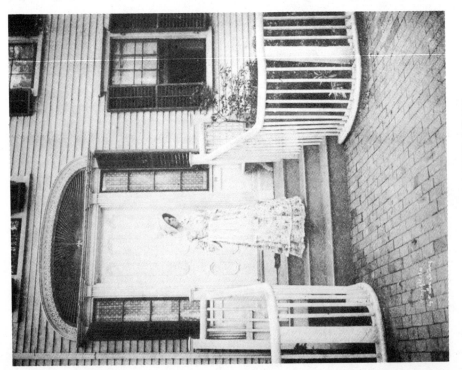

JANE OF NANTUCKET

Beautifully spiraled toasters, now so much sought, held the bread upright on the hearth. Revolving broilers with serpentine grills and all manner of fantastic shapes were used for steaks. Birds were spitted and revolved from a swivel hook one of which we show. The hob, so common in England, was scarcely used, at least in the North. The English fashion of swinging a diminutive crane from a high andiron, a most picturesque and attractive device, we have not seen as yet in this country.

The great mass of the fireplace, when thoroughly heated, acted somewhat as the huge porcelain German stoves of this generation. The heat was retained and diffused through the night, and though the frost line might approach within several feet of the blaze the room was fairly well tempered.

An ideal modern dining room is secured by the restoration of such an old kitchen retaining every quaint and ancient feature with dressers and open shelves and wall hooks to exhibit the pride of the housewife.

OLD FASHIONED GABLES

WE have scattered through our pages various sketches of ancient roof lines in Nantucket and elsewhere. The outline here of a gambrel, there of a pointed roof, there of a lean-to, and various combinations or ranks of these shapes as they range back, one behind the other, when one looks down upon an ancient town, constitutes its chief charm when seen as a whole. Peeping through the branches of lofty trees or half hidden behind one another they call out protective and homing instincts. These roofs are best seen, perhaps, in Siasconset, though some Cape villages afford fine groupings of this sort.

On the North Shore one sees statelier three story houses, as in Salem and Newburyport. They are of a later and more pretentious period but in their ample size remind us of the large families then prevalent. Containing as they did twelve rooms and three great hall-ways, besides, often, a series of side halls, they were almost institutions in themselves. In the typical house there was no L. On one side there was the dining room and kitchen and on the other the front and back parlors with eight chambers on the two stories above.

The outlines of a detached homestead are often sufficiently alluring to detain us. There seemed to be a feeling that if one wanted room the thing to do was to build on rather than to repair whatever existed. The writer remembers many times in his childhood hearing farmers say " It is not worth repair " of some old shed. Instead, however, of removing that shed, another was added to it and we recollect houses on which five generations, at least, have tried their hand until the result is a marvelous up and down and in and out and back and forth of roof line. If these lines are softened by overhanging trees they are often very graceful. Otherwise they cause us to lament the lack of unity. That very lack, however, to some minds constitutes a charm. There is at Hanover Four Corners a house said to have three stories on one floor. It is all, indeed, built upon the ground, but on a declivity so that one goes up and down stairs to three levels, which are, nevertheless, all on the lower story.

Novelists have ever raved over rambling houses. They are, indeed, wonderful for children who would play hide and seek and rummage among the shed roofs of the successive disorders of architecture. If such old gables are crowned with stately chimneys and none of your modern spindling affairs that disgrace the name, their outlines are very satisfactory. The coloring of the old brick, mingled with the gray-green of old shingles and topping some weathered gable that has met successfully the storms of two hundred New England winters, creates an ensemble capable of enthralling the traveler.

We asked at such a house, " Have you had many opportunities to sell? " " Every week," was the reply, " through the season, ve are besought to dispose of the place." No longer need we be anxious regarding the tumbled-down farmsteads of New England. Our only anxiety will be to secure the wherewithal to purchase them. Yet when all is said there

PITTSFIELD FIELD ROAD

THE DREAMY SHORE—NORFOLK COUNTY

THE MANSE GARDEN — STOCKBRIDGE

ENTERING THE STOCKBRIDGE LINKS

NANTUCKET ROOF LINES

are many owners who will neither sell nor restore but allow their old homes to fall about their ears. It is another proof that one's own interest cannot be trusted as a sufficient stimulus to care for one's property.

We still more fear the spirit of modernizing or repairing old houses. Already most of them have been ruined by such processes undertaken without knowledge, taste or sentiment. There are literally thousands of instances in which persons with more money than discretion have repaired, restored, enlarged and decorated until there is not a square inch visible of any old surface and until the original builder would fail to recognize his child or would have felt disgraced by it. We have in mind now a Massachusetts town of twenty thousand people with only two dwellings left of a quaint, early character.

SOME COUNTRY COTTAGES

M ASSACHUSETTS, There She Stands! " The title of our picture (p. 160) may serve as a winning type of a country setting. The curve of the road throws the house directly ahead as one approaches it, a very important and often forgotten landscape feature.

The great ash tree to the left, from which an unsightly dead limb was removed for this picture, provides just the right flanking border which also arches the road. The old red house on a quiet road almost speaks to us of its successive occupants and is a kind of living monument.

The Fairbanks homestead at Dedham is too well known to delay us long (p. 211). It is surprising that it should be so difficult to provide for the upkeep of this ancient house with the quaintest roof line in Massachusetts.

The Leominster cottage (p. 212) removed from the highway like a nest of a robin, loving yet fearing the step of man, has caught our eye for many years. The Mission House at Stockbridge (p. 179), though without the great central chimney, is, as seen under the magnificent sweep of its protecting foliage, thoroughly satisfactory. In the process of time perhaps it may be restored to its earlier condition. Externally its beautiful door head is about all that is left as it was.

In " Fair Old Sudbury " (p. 183) is an illustration of the effectiveness of the apple tree about the front of the dwelling. Here a rural highway gives the vista, and the arch of the blossoms is good, over the road and the hidden dwelling. It is a kind of natural setting, doubtless not planned but felt, and far more appealing in an artistic way, than something that has been arranged consciously.

At " Meerholm," Siasconset (p. 152), the appeal of a miniature effect in a cottage is secured. The open space above the door is doubtless covered in summer by a rolling canvas, a very effective method of securing shade when one wants it and dispensing with it on dull days.

" A Cottage Through the Cornfield " (p. 119) appeals to the sense of plenty especially when, as in this instance, the shocks are large and the dwelling appears small. The persons who cultivate these fields have held them for many generations and made good against the New England weather, have educated their children, have led in the direction of town affairs and evidenced to the world that a man may still dwell on his acres, even in eastern Massachusetts, and gain all that is worth while.

A STERN SHORE—GLOUCESTER

A LITTLE HOMESTEAD—SHREWSBURY

EAST HAVERHILL

MEERHOLM—NANTUCKET

Cottage decoration is seen carried to its fullest extent on page 139 where Nantucket maidens chat at the gate. The porch here is beautifully effective. Above is seen the platform where the housewives watched for the return of their husbands from whaling voyages.

GARDENS

MASSACHUSETTS is particularly rich in gardens but there is not in the usual garden the individuality required for pictorial effects. A few like that of the Samoset Garden in Plymouth are set forth. Another aspect appears on page 168.

"A Pembroke Garden" (p. 248) is a pleasing glimpse of a garden that has run to riot, with a mellow shingled dwelling beyond. We have already referred to Plymouth gardens.

Gardening has ever been a favorite avocation of clergymen and "The Manse Garden at Stockbridge" (p. 148), looking out over Monument Mountain, is a very successful instance of clerical gardening.

Of course, the fashionable hollyhock must figure largely in modern gardens, and this is an instance in which fashion and good taste meet. The large, individual flowers, like hollyhocks, are far more effective than small flowers. The fashion of fencing in a little enclosure in the front of the house, as on page 151, has gone out with the necessity for it, but its charm remains.

A child wandering in a garden is singularly appropriate, as we associate the freshness of the flowers with innocence and youth, as in "Elizabeth in Her Garden" (p. 56).

The large formal gardens of the North Shore and the Berkshires are many of them very stately and impressive but we have not thought them as important to represent, since we try to avoid for the most part any formal or modern effects in this work, seeking rather the quaint and early flavor of Massachusetts life.

The garden of the Wayside Inn (p. 171) is very excellent on account of the end of its vista, a gable being more satisfactory than the side of a dwelling.

The blooms that huddle about the little wayside cottage on the Mohawk Trail (p. 288) do so much at relieving the bareness of life that we wonder we do not see them everywhere.

THE CULTURED TRAMP

SEEKING beauty spots off the Mohawk Trail we came upon a little nook beside a field road. It was sheltered from the wind, hidden from the highway, looked out on a fair valley, was warm, beautiful and secret. Here we discovered an oven built up of field stones, and all the apparatus of a tramp's paradise. The irresponsibility of tramping is its probable appeal to so many. The tramp lets the world wag. He toils not neither does he spin nor gather into barns. Not, indeed, that we would liken him precisely to a lily, especially to a white one, but life seems to be sweet to him. His only dinner bell is the sense of hunger and his alarm clock is the sun shining in his face on a summer morning. The fisherman shares in some of the tramp's joys; also the canoeist and the walking tourist. With some modifications the tramp's life should appeal to many of us. If we eliminate its bold beggary, its other aspects open the world to us in many ways more intimately than could a limousine. Lying under a tree we absorb knowledge willy-nilly, of a kind that it is good to have.

Anybody who would eat luncheon indoors during a summer journey in the country fails of his rights. He is forsaking the charms spread for his delectation. It is, we may fairly say, possible to tramp though using an automobile. It means frequent stops and side excursions on foot. The return to the car and departure from it have their pleasures vastly enhanced by the contrast.

GOLDEN BIRCHES—CONCORD

APPLE TREE BEND — HARVARD

RIVULETS OF FOAM — NORTH SHORE

A RAINBOW ROOF, QUINCY

On an October morning if we climb the pasture slopes of Warren we have enough of the world at our feet to fill the eye and the heart. The air is sweet with autumn scents and rustles crooningly in the maple leaves above us. The curious calves approach, their moist muzzles thrust forward in the hope that we have brought them something. A squirrel scolds us from the limb above. A chipmunk, like the shadow of a leaf, rushes across a ledge of rock. A wise old crow mocks us from a tall pine. The shadows of the clouds pass mystically over the Quabaug, the meadow and the southern hills. The cornfields ripple and whisper of their plenty. The orchard hangs full with rich, red Baldwins and yellow Bellflowers. A rambling stone wall, built by a returning soldier of the Revolution and repaired by all the generations of his children, separates our pasture from the orchard. In it there is a bar-way with old mortised posts covered with lichen and greenish gray in the orchard shadow. A spring with a tub set around it, a little below us, sends its overflow down the run under the road to the river. The roof lines of the farm houses are partly hidden and partly shown through the elm tops. The world is thoroughly good.

It feeds our imagination, our sense of romance, our present need, our love for protection. It invites the roving foot and calls irresistibly by its distant curving roads and waving tree tops.

Whatever truth is in evolution it has increased our sense of unity with the sod beneath us and the air about us. The knowledge that we have come so far is the most splendid promise that we shall go on, and the airplane that loses itself above us makes us brothers to the eagle and familiars of the storm. Life is widening and deepening and enriching. It is full enough and has a sufficient number of undiscovered treasures and glories to challenge a superlative genius. Yet it is a tender and wise mother to our more ordinary and limited intelligence. We find on this pasture side all that we want and more than we need and we see an outline of a limitless human movement.

We must so far play on the sod and with the loam; so far wander into the forests; so far wade in the brook as to keep our joy in contact with our old world.

THE SCIENCE OF AN OUTDOOR LUNCHEON

WE gaze in wonder, as we tour, at the numerous motors drawn up by the side of a great thoroughfare, while their occupants eat luncheon. There in the midst of the noise and dust their outlook is unsightly. Yet they are content. How little it requires to please! The science of a luncheon en route is a nice study. One should begin a half hour beforehand to look for an inviting lane or a little used highway. Drawing off then to the side of a brook where the grass is green and there is no sound save the current on the pebbles or the call of the birds, we may spread our feast by the side of the bole of an aged oak. The brook causes a gentle breeze under the branches and the minnows rise for the crumbs that we scatter in the shallows. This is your little world for the time being. You own everything you can take in of the many shades of green that spread their living lace on the margin of the rivulet.

THE SILVER SAFE—LEE MANSION

BERKSHIRE BLOSSOMS

"MASSACHUSETTS, THERE SHE STANDS!"—FRAMINGHAM

A DUXBURY HOMESTEAD

For you is all this beauty, unrecorded by others, unappreciated by the rushing crowd, the murmur of whose passage is dully heard in the distance.

Of course, a bite into the segment of a piece of squash pie under these circumstances has a flavor unmatched elsewhere. One may even, as some farmer was accused by his scandalized wife of doing, eat his pie backwards. The crusty corner is a particularly tasty bite. But then, one is not confined to this historic and little understood diet. Although Emerson ate it for breakfast and it became responsible for his brilliant essays, persons of alleged culture have been known to sniff at it. A near sniff, however, ends in surrender.

A doughnut with a hole in the middle is, as no one can deny, a curve of beauty. We have eaten enough such doughnuts including a few of a freakish twisted curve to be filled in our dreams with Gothic wheels, spirals and arches, not to say with gargoyles.

By the edge of the wood there are red checkerberries and their tender green leaves that give tang to the luncheon. One might even chew a bit of sorrel if hard put to it.

A retreat like this has better artistic outlines than those shown by Corot. His district was rather flat and comparatively unattractive. We have something here besides what the Dutch pictures have rendered immortal. Chase and Inness have known their opportunity and in time all will follow them, as the wise are already doing. The English people enjoy a luncheon in the country and Americans, in spite of their multifarious touring, are too often on their way to places perhaps better avoided.

The conditions of our climate do not always invite us out of doors, although it is a pleasure to fight the storm, but when we do find nature in a kindly mood let us by no means miss in America the wonderful charm of out of doors. Of course all thinking persons realize that this charm is not much known or felt. Witness the long row of sitters on a hotel porch. Witness the swarms in the public places of the cities even in summer. Try this test: ask two or three people at random on every street corner for a direction to some public edifice. You will find that probably half of them are strangers who came from nowhere and are going on to another nowhere. The average man lacks an aim. What does he know about the friendly crook of an elm branch? Why are poets rare? It is not a lack of intellectual power but a lack of feeling. Given the passion for anything and expression will follow. Find a new place to eat luncheon every day during the vacation season and write them all, each on its page, in your book of records. In a few years you will have, as you review your notes, a multitude of comforting or amusing or inspiring allusions. Of

LANCASTER WATERS

DECORATIONS OF AN OLD WALL—WORCESTER COUNTY

DOVER WATERS

A COCHITUATE CAUSEWAY

numerous crusades of reform what more important than this, to enrich the common life now so wretchedly poor, meagre and bare. An anchorite of the rocky desert has a wider range of imagination than many a dweller in a stately home.

BEAUTY SPOTS

HERE and there we have been impressed by some great tree or a fine stream or a noble outlook and we mention a few of these: As one goes into Canton from Norwood there is an old world viaduct crossing a corner of the pool. This combination always catches the eye, reminding one a little of the charms of Chenonceaux. Apparently nobody planned to secure this little setting, a statement that we suppose is true of almost all such places. Curiously enough the conscious work of man in creating beauty spots can never escape the mark of sophistication.

As one goes south from Stoughton through the Eastons, the Ames estates in the flowering season give much charm to the roadside.

Through the woods to Wareham from the north, following here and there the side roads, one finds much to enjoy.

Southerly from Taunton, following the west bank of the Taunton River to Dighton and Dighton Rock and thence on through Somerset to the environs of Fall River, various water glimpses of a pleasing character are opened.

On the Connecticut River starting from Holyoke and running to Mount Tom and thence leaving Easthampton on the west and hugging the base of the Holyoke range, one may go on to Ox Bow and circle right, coming back past Smith's Ferry to Holyoke. On this ride one will get many a broad mountain and river glimpse well worth dwelling upon.

Crossing the river at Holyoke to South Hadley Falls and thence to South Hadley through the Notch to Amherst, North Amherst and Sunderland one has much of the fair plains region of the Connecticut. At

Sunderland one crosses the river to South Deerfield, and this short stretch affords a fine view of South and North Sugar Loaf, at the bridge. One may then turn from South Deerfield to the Conway road, which is attractive, into Ashfield, one of the towns set on a hill and long a summer literary shrine, thence through Buckland to Shelburne Falls where one meets the Mohawk Trail.

The views from the trail westward from Shelburne Falls are, while very extensive, more pleasing to view than to picture, owing to their very extent. The outlook into the valley of Adams from the summit is one of the finest in the state, especially when the cloud rack stretches its changing canopy above.

From Greenfield one may make a delightful circuit to Northfield through Turner's Falls and may return through Miller's Falls. The last of the route is the least interesting. A recently improved road from Greenfield over the trail via Greenfield Mountain and Shelburne to Shelburne Falls will inevitably stimulate one to select summer sites on fine, strategic outlooks. If one could only follow the river back from Shelburne Falls to Greenfield he would get some of the best water views in the state, but the country is almost too rough to permit such a road being built. One can only come down to the river here and there on side roads as at Bardwell's Ferry.

From Littleton to Groton and Townsend through Ashby to Ashburnham one finds highlands with laurel, balsamy woodlands, little lakes and mountain outlooks.

Going on thence to Winchendon one may swing back to Baldwinsville, Templeton and Gardner. The route from Templeton or Gardner through Hubbardston to Princeton is not as well known as most of our roads, but with Wachusett always ahead or at some angle of beauty, the road has its charms.

HIGHLAND BLOSSOMS — BUCKLAND

SPRING HARMONY — FRAMINGHAM

OVER THE ORCHARD—FRANKLIN COUNTY

LARKSPUR GARDEN—PLYMOUTH

PLACE NAMES IN MASSACHUSETTS

THE struggles, the weariness and even the theology of the settlers were reflected in their place names. Of course the names were transferred, largely, from English recollections. But others speak more of the experiences, the journeys and the beliefs of the people. For instance, Tophet Swamp in Carlisle is almost as expressive for Massachusetts as Hell's Half Acre is in the Yellowstone.

Heart Break Hill, just out of Ipswich, speaks for itself, and in this connection we may mention Break Neck Hill, in Freetown.

Half Way Brook, Nine Mile Pond, Five Mile Pond, Four Mile Pond, and Middletown indicate journeying appellations.

Moses Hill in Manchester reminds one of the law of the colonies. Even Mount Ararat in Millbury was not forgotten.

Labor in Vain Creek near Ipswich certainly affords fun to this generation though we doubt if it was applied in humor. One would almost think that Bunyan named the natural features of the state. Indeed, he did through those who read him.

Golden Cove Brook in Chelmsford is a touch of sunshine. Providence Hill near Westford indicates that Massachusetts did not give up wholly to Roger Williams its serene faith. Conscience Hills in Tyngsboro is of puzzling application, but Snake Meadow Hill near by we can understand.

Anybody who has worked through the woods to follow a direction toward a lake will understand how Sought For Pond came to be named. Abram's Hill is also in Tyngsboro. Rockbottom is a hard name for a village but a good foundation for Pilgrim life. Ghost Hill in Northboro, a little to the south of Mount Pisgah, is expressive but perhaps no more so than Sulphur Hill which is close adjoining. Neither was Mount Nebo forgotten, near Medfield.

Stirrup Brook is not an uncommon name; whether it means that one waded to the stirrup or lost that important aid to a traveler we do not know. But why Knickup Hill in Wrentham or Stop River in Norfolk?

Hopping Brook in Holliston is easy. Wrangling Brook in Groton evidently commemorates some border-line squabble and Witch Brook in Townsend brings back old memories. Spectacle Pond is often repeated, being applied to two oval bodies of water near together. Hell Pond is a hard name for a fair town like Harvard, as also is Purgatory Chasm in Sutton.

The various Rattle Snake Hills or Mountains, Bear Hills, Fox Brooks, Wild Cat Hills, Wolf Ponds and Hartlands remind one of the " varmints " and the game which our fathers fought or hunted, and Trap Fall Brook, Ashby, is a reminiscence. Nineteenth Hill in Winchendon indicates that somebody was simple enough to try to count the hills in Massachusetts, on his route, a thing which he evidently gave up.

We do not understand such names as Wine Brook nor Burned Shirt River, near Hubbardston. Bean Porridge Hill west of Fitchburg is no joke. Bloody Brook in Deerfield was named for the great massacre.

The naming of mountains from their shapes was common enough like Sugar Loaf in Deerfield, Peaked Mountain near Monson, Dumpling Mountain near Palmer, Doublet Hill in Weston, Horse Mountain near Hatfield, and Bald Hills are repeated all over New England.

Devil's Garden in the Notch of Granby is altogether too near Mount Holyoke College, it being on the way thence to Amherst College, but Bachelor Brook in South Hadley is better.

Streams named from their color as Red, Muddy or Black Brook or Green Pond are found. Names that are merely comical without apparent meaning occur occasionally like Mount Terrydiddle in Rehoboth just above Bad Luck Brook.

On the coast near Rockport a shoal is called Twopenny Loaf whether in derision or from the shape we cannot say, but Coffin's Beach adjoining is from the name of a man. Folly Cove near Rockport is one of those delusive entrances which afford no real protection against the northern gales. Ten Pound and Five Pound Islands in Gloucester harbor are familiar to the public, and also more sadly known is Norman's Woe.

GARDEN OF THE WAYSIDE INN

BILLOWS OF BLOSSOMS—FRANKLIN COUNTY

A HOPKINTON FIRESIDE

WHISPERING GRASSES NEAR ASHBY

Clam Pudding Pond in Plymouth probably refers to a Pilgrim picnic. Does Moon Shine Hill in Buckland mean anything more than a silvery gleam? Perhaps Bread and Cheese Brook indicated the point where luncheon was served to men, just at Baiting Brook showed where the horse got his mid-day portion.

Trouble with the Indians was reflected in Heathen Meadow Brook, Indian Head Hill, Wigwam Hill and similar names.

Mount Lizzie was named before the little automobile tried to climb it, but Brimstone Hill in Ware yet gives off its aroma.

Someone has written an entertaining book on names of persons. We have only to suggest here that Adam, when he named the animals, knocked off work too soon. It would have added not a little to the joy and beauty of life had we employed him in advance to name the places and the persons of the world out into which he was to go.

APPROACHES

THE ancients very wisely gave much attention to approaches. In fact, the approach was more than half of all in the effect of architecture especially as when one arrived there was so little to find, — merely an inner shrine perhaps. In domestic architecture and landscape effects, the approach of a country place is its making.

In " Up The Lane " (p. 72) we have a curving country road which really has no connection by ownership with the house, it being the crosscut at a V of two roads. Nevertheless, as one goes up this lane toward the house it has the effect of a private approach and in things of this sort it is effect that counts.

If one can get an approach under a huge limb of a noble tree like that on page 91 it is something to be arranged.

The approach to Wayside Inn shown on page 127 is one of the best among the simpler places of the country.

Perhaps there is no appeal out of doors equal to that afforded by the changing scenes on a wisely calculated drive.

Such effects cannot be obtained, as a rule, with old houses, because they too often hug the road closely. It is frequently feasible to get an old road vacated as a public highway, where a dwelling is situated amongst the hills or away from general traffic. We have an instance in mind where an old highway, narrow and winding, was discontinued by the town and taken over by the owner of a dwelling upon it. He then had the seclusion of a country drive and all his guests experienced a pleasure far greater than could be secured by a new drive.

Such a drive is made many times more effective if it crosses a brook, on a curve if possible, the small stone arches of the bridge and the water effects adding to the composition. Some of these features are secured in " As it was in 1700 " (p. 247) and " Newburyport Turnpike " (p. 259).

Aside from the beauty secured by an approach to a country dwelling there is the convenience of having one's abode in the midst of one's acres so that on every hand there may be features of economic or esthetic interest, — here a cornfield; there waving grain; at the left a clump of maples; at the right a stream; on the north a wooded hill; on the south the gardens. There is no reason why the Japanese should, with their more limited opportunities, so far surpass us. Give them a little plot of ground and a stream anywhere near and they will create a water garden fascinating beyond measure. Our English friends have carried out the thought of water gardens but in a manner too formal for simple country homes. We need, merely, to help nature a little and not completely to tame her.

Given a brook, trees and uneven ground, a little paradise may be created anywhere. Water always speaks of wealth and plenty. For the Orientals anywhere it made a garden.

The drive first following a brook, then climbing a gentle declivity, then skirting along a somewhat elevated bank, then curving between fine trees and stone walls, not too fresh and perfect, leads us to new delights with

MAYNARD WATERING PLACE   NINE MILE POND

PIE FROM THE OLD OVEN — COOPER-AUSTIN HOUSE

THE GOULDING HOMESTEAD — SOUTH SUDBURY

AN ORCHARD HOMESTEAD

every turn of the wheel. The architect is at last consulted but the land-scapist almost never. His work is something that the owner feels he can do without. Of the two, however, we think that the setting of a home is more important than the edifice itself.

We have dragged into this book one picture from Rhode Island (p. 226) for the reason that we have no such dwelling in Massachusetts now, and Rhode Island, though perhaps not to be included in our Series, has supplied us with several remarkable seventeenth century features of architecture of entrancing interest. A dwelling like this Rhode Island example would be impoverished, artistically, if it lacked its ivy. There are certain combinations that are irresistible. The Preservation Society is to be congratulated on the acquisition of this remarkable dwelling, the best of this class of the half dozen or so.

At Cohasset fine advantage has been taken of a rocky island as a summer place. An appropriate bridge spans the narrow chasm between the island and the main land and the approach is well nigh perfect. The shore districts of Massachusetts afford a great many sites which, in one way or another, could be made thoroughly attractive.

The " little house by the side of the road " has, we know, its merits and its call but we are learning these days that if we are to do any thinking we must get out of the road. One vehicle is a good deal like another and merely to see the world go by, though the procession may make a wonderful little poem, is not especially stimulating to the intellect. This reminds us that the best things in Massachusetts are perhaps not to be seen on the road at all. A motor boat or even a row boat will reveal more, probably, of artistic curves and banks decorated with arches of branches than a similar distance on a highway.

The use of islands in lakes, as dwellings, has received little attention. Every island of any elevation is, when reached, a site of great merit. If the waters that approach it are shoal a causeway may be built. If it lies near the shore a bridge may be thrown to it, but if somewhat removed from the main land an arrangement of keeping the noise and bother of a garage far from the dwelling at the main land end and a connection by motor boat is very appealing to the sense of independence. An island is a little world. There a few sheep may be allowed to wander over all the grounds and dispense with any need of fences or lawn mowers. Many English parks are kept in beautiful condition in this manner.

We show a camp on Lake Quinsigamond. We wonder why it is just a camp and not a home for eight months of the year.

Massachusetts has many hundreds of lakes of such a size that a single farm often goes all about one. The charm of " The Lady of the Lake " has appealed to everyone. How much this charm arises from the fact that the dwelling was on an island few have considered. The moated effects of the earlier European dwellings were artistic to a degree. It would sometime be feasible with far less expense than is freely put out on useless walls to impound a body of water about a knoll and secure a country place, distinctive, enchanting and secluded yet not out of sight of the public.

There are many regions on the north shore and about our rivers like the Assabet or the Sudbury that would lend themselves happily to such effects. The impounding of waters amongst the hills is increasing the opportunities of this sort. Whether one likes deep waters and bold sky outlines or the fen country of the eastern portion of the state, there is something to please every cultivated taste. We have in mind now an es-

NEPONSET WATERS

THE MISSION HOUSE—STOCKBRIDGE

MEADOW ARCHES — LANCASTER

LYNN MARSHES

tate on which a vast fortune has been expended, with a very lofty and ornate iron fence on each side of the highway which passes through the acreage. How much better to have expended this effort on a site which required no such prison-like cutting off!

The old Choate place on the north shore is an island domain not yet spoiled by overmuch attention. We mention it because it often happens that too much is done in the way of precision and careful finish of approaches. People are putting cobble stone in their dwellings and cut stones in their walls, whereas they should reverse the process, as there scarcely ever was known a cut stone wall and there never was known a cobble stone house in the ancient New England days. It is far easier to learn the orders of architecture than it is to harmonize one's plan with the region and to place one's home so that it may appear as a part of the landscape.

On each side of the front door of a country place we often find beautiful elms. As twins they embellish the approach and lend it majesty. Even better than that they are connected with an ancient custom and have become monuments of romance. We have noted instances where the bride and the groom on their wedding day planted the youthful and slender trees which have gone on together until they afford a shelter to the aged couple and to their children after them to the third and fourth generation.

There comes to our mind a curving embankment across a depression through which a brook ran. The curve was so gentle and so neatly marked by ribbons of turf and so fairly shaded by rows of elms that the little brick gable of the homestead as it came into view was wonderfully effective. Yet all this was a very small farm place. It had no pretension to wealth or display. We have never seen anything better of its kind. This was probably the effect of unconscious adaptation. Hence the charm.

A NORTH SHORE KITCHEN

THE TIN PEDLER

TO CHILDREN living in the country a generation since, the arrival of the tin pedler was the most important event of the month. He had a very large cart generally painted red, that had faded to a mellow tint. It was full of wonderful drawers on every side which were revealed when its doors were opened. What treasures were disclosed from these drawers! We children stood, all agog, with eyes like saucers. To us that pedler's cart was the Pandora's box of every conceivable joy. It was a small dry goods and notion store, a hardware shop and a little of almost everything else. Brooms stood in a rack at one corner and huge bundles of rags which had been taken in barter were tied on top and held in by a dainty little rack, for be it known unto this generation that the

BERKSHIRE MOUNTAIN BROOK — WORONOKO

FAIR OLD SUDBURY

ABOVE THE BROOK—WELLESLEY

pedler's cart was a work of art.   It was graced by a fine goose neck front, and, like an epic poem, it had a beginning, a middle and an end.   We were especially eager to get a few tin dishes and small shovels for the child's garden.   Not much money passed in these transactions but while paper was still made from rags a big bag of clippings and discarded garments would purchase quite a quantity of hardware with a few spools of thread and papers of pins.

The pedler himself was almost as interesting as his cargo.   He was lean and long as the ancient mariner and most likely was old.   He drove a good horse for the load was heavy.   How he ever lived was a mystery, but he lived well and always knew at what farm to stop for dinner.   At one time the pedler's cart was an important institution being, in one instance, sent out in great numbers by a wholesale merchant.

The old pedler often talked to himself as people who are alone are in the habit of doing.   It is a good habit.   They always have attentive listeners and are never interrupted nor are they ever subject to dispute. Like the philosophers they are least alone when alone.   We have heard of late some rumor of the revival, in the form of a glorified gasoline wagon, of the pedler's cart.   There is no reason why it should not bring Paris to every door!   It was only twenty years ago that we actually found on the road the tin pedler (p. 132), but so far as our recent experience is concerned he is as extinct as the passenger pigeon.

ASKING DIRECTIONS

THE old joke in the almanac fifty years ago ran:
" Boy, where does this road go to? "
" Don't go no where as I know's on."
The information extracted from this juvenile philosopher is about as satisfactory as the average.

Lost in a maze of the Worcester county hills at a crossing of two roads within a few rods of another turn, with not a house in sight, we start on what seems to the charioteer the probable direction. "That can't be right," says the fair passenger. We throw a veil over the remainder of the discussion. When one is weary or ripe for a little sharp argument what is better to set one off than a difference of opinion on two roads, when information is scant and opinion strong?

It requires a mile's run to reach a small farmhouse. The front door is never opened, apparently. On the way to the back door a large and somewhat uncertain dog is met. The usual hypocrisy of " good doggy! " follows. We find a lonely woman who is pleased with the sight of human kind. The unfortunate investigation begins. We wish to go to a point beyond her knowledge and the points within her knowledge we know nothing of, so that minds do not meet.

The best way to Ware is the first left hand road after you pass a right hand road. That is, you do not take the narrow road into the woods but the first wide left hand road. You go down over the hill until you come to the school house and you take the middle road there. When you come to a bridge you do not cross it but you keep straight ahead on this side of the river, and then you had better inquire again.

Is there anything more humiliating than to ask a direction and within twenty rods be at a divergence of opinion as to whether we were told to turn to the right or to the left? We have personally tested a great many fellow travelers and we find that it is seldom they agree on the directions given.

What is a road? After two or three miles we see a man ploughing. We walk across the ploughed field. You know how it is. The dirt fills into your shoes even when you do not go over them. You ask for enlightenment. You learn you should have taken another road two miles back. " But," you object, " We were told to take the first left hand." " Oh, well, that was not a road and that did not count." By this time, as you go back to your vehicle, you are informed that of course you were wrong all the time. But what is there about traveling by motor that

MANCHESTER ARCHES

UNLOADING AT THE STACK — CAPE COD

BURLINGTON BIRCHES

WATERING TROUGH — BERKSHIRE

keeps us from going back? We had rather go around over half of the state of Massachusetts. This is not obstinacy but enterprise, and a desire to explore. Who knows what beauties lie over the top of the hill?

By this time the road is springy and rocky and narrow. You hear an inquiry, " What would you do if you met a car? " Anybody who imagines that there is not mystery and variety, romance and heroism, to be had on an exploring trip does not understand hill roads and human nature.

After about eight miles we seem to be on familiar ground and find ourselves at a corner where we diverged. This is comforting because we are on the right road now, only we are going in the *wrong direction* and have been for three miles!

Never mind, we have seen a part of Massachusetts that no wise man ever saw. A gem of a landscape may reveal itself almost anywhere and from what unpromising material pearls are made!

In a western Massachusetts village we wish to see an object of interest at the public library. We are told that Aunt Jane Jones used to have the key. She lived in the cottage beyond the church. Aunt Jane said " No, Hepsy Hunt now kept the key, in the last house in the village on the left." Hepsy was away from home but out back of the barn the hired man told us that he did not know where that key was now, but he more than half believed they had it up at the grocery store. There we are told that it had been too much trouble and they kind of thought the minister had it, but he was out of town today. We still wish to find that key and we mean to do so on the next visit to the town.

And that leads us to enter a little upon the ways and means of obtaining pictures of the country.

PICTURE GLEANING

THE fisherman goes out in the hope that he may bring something back. If he is so fortunate as to secure a perch he has to do something with it yet, which is not so agreeable. Fishing for pictures is a diversion which appeals to many persons. There are supposed to be in the neighborhood of twenty million cameras in our broad land and there are probably at least nineteen million persons who privately think, and not so privately either, that they can make just as good pictures as anybody. They like to show these pictures.

The question what will interest does not enter into the discussion. It is taken for granted that the multitudinous attitudes of Mary's baby, fore and aft, larboard and starboard, or keeled over are all fascinating. If it were not for babies, what would become of the camera trade?

Then there is the picture of the family in the new car at the door. To be sure, the car is just like every other car and the door, unhappily, is just like any door. If all the falsehoods told about pictures are laid up against us — but then, there would not be space to write them all.

A good picture is, doubtless, worth while for the satisfaction of the person who obtains it as well as for others. The certain test of its quality is difficult to apply, but popularity is at least a sign that others agree with us. Be slow, gentle reader, to say that it is easy to find good pictures. Composition seems easy like all other work when it is successful. It is a subtle question, what constitutes sufficient importance to be worth recording in the composition?

Often one knows on the instant that a thing is good. We remember a beeline that we once made across two states for one picture when we knew all things were in their prime and the setting was complete. It was better than a myriad of ordinary pictures.

A picture near Pittsfield (p. 147) we waited to obtain standing with bulb in hand from five o'clock in the morning until eleven. Not a moment in that time was there a lull in a furious wind. Even so, we do not claim

THE WEALTH OF MAY — WARE

FARING TOWARD WACHUSETT

SHREWSBURY BIRCHES

HOLLYHOCK ROW — HAVERHILL

A MIDDLESEX LEAN-TO

that the result was altogether satisfactory. What is so cold as early morning cold in the summer with a white frost and a long excursion before breakfast? For it is often the case that pictures must be had near sunrise, if ever. Then, perhaps, there is silence. Those rare days when the quiet of five o'clock and the tender greens of spring coincide, and you have reached the beauty spot, are never forgotten.

On one occasion a sturdy farmer came out to a bridge where we were looking down a brook with our camera, and asked us what we were looking at. We told him we were surveying for a new railroad but he did not seem to believe it. Thus information is often wasted. Another day in the long drive approaching a hill farm we were endeavoring to record the exquisite beauty of a great crabapple tree in its lucious prime.

The genial owner of the farm with his wife came out full of curiosity to know what we should do with the picture. For one thing, we should send them a copy. It had never impressed them as anything unusual but it was a fair and rare vision, the turfy road beneath it being covered with its May snows. It is clearly improper for us to state which picture in this volume records the incident, but now we have established a warm friendship with the family. They believe it the beauty of their home. They understand it to be something worth the pause of a traveler. Its setting has somewhat lifted their thoughts now that they come to have its beauty endorsed. Thus some men never know how beautiful their wives are until they hear it outside. It is so much better to know without being told, but better to be told than not to know.

CURIOUS ITEMS

OLD Washington Piccard rebottoms chairs, gathers the flags in the full of the August moon, and insures lasting qualities by carrying them through the doorway to his house, cut end first. In gathering them he excludes the female flags." Anyway, the chair bottoms lasted a hundred years, if properly used. But he should have cut them in June.

An old Newbury house had an iron rigging just inside the front door for lowering heavy valuables into a secret cellar beneath the floor of the front hall. Secret panels in walls the usual device of romantic novelists were not rare in reality. Secret passages in chimneys seem ever to fascinate explorers. A dwelling near the Newburyport Turnpike has lately been found to contain in its chimney an ancient room with the furniture intact. [*See page* 198.]

BERKSHIRE BROOK—LANESBORO

WILMINGTON SHADOWS

THORN TREES — BOSTON

SNOW COVERED PINES — NEEDHAM

MAN AND THE STORM

When the sharp blast falls from mountain walls,
    And swirls o'er the winter plain,
And weaves its woof over fence and roof,
In a blanket without stain,
Oh, then to tramp that snow-raised ramp!
Oh, then for the stiffening fight!
The February gale may hurl its hail,
    We breast it with our might!

Oh! what are your palms and your silken calms,
    Oh! what are your southern skies
To the half-hid rills and the snow-crowned hills,
When the wild cloud past them flies?
We exult in the death of the winter's breath,
When the twilight softly falls.
For we storm the snow when high drifts blow,
    And deep unto deep still calls!

The men who dwell where moor and fell
    Are buried beneath the blast,
These are the men who tame the fen
And lift up the homes that last!
The life is nil without the will
Steeled to an iron grasp,
For the soul is as high as the northern sky,
    And the heart exceeds its task.

The town crier of Ipswich is said to have uttered this jingle after every ringing of his bell:

> " Run rogues, run,
> The court's begun,
> Stand before the justice,
> And tell what you've done."

Some villages are said to have revived the custom of the town crier and we believe in one or two instances, perhaps in Nantucket, the custom never fully went out. It was a good method not only of disseminating general news but was useful for advertising and in this way eked out the scanty honorarium of the crier.

The rag rug is in certain districts of New England beautifully made but in other parts it is wretchedly done. We once had a letter from a woman of the wilds describing the sort of rags which she preferred. She said, " Shirtes do not make very good rages. Vestes are no good for rages. But pantes make very good rages." And yet it was not an angry letter.

Having occasion for a bee expert we wrote to a gentleman known to be skilful, asking his assistance. We received a letter which has been much prized: " In several ways word has been brought to me that you wanted your bees overhawled and set up right. Twice I have been very nearly stung to death and there are very risky chances for me to run. I swore against the business quite a while ago. I will try to say now that I will not answer any call or calls to work with the Bees. Stinging is very painful and dangerous to me, and so far as I know there is not any law that compells me or any other person to run any risk simply because moneyed man requests and demands it. I have told everyone for the past 7 years I should not work at bees to please anyone. I have the constitutional right to work or refuse to work at anything that is injurious to me in every way. Mr. —— attempted to dictate to me yesterday that I should go to do your work regardless of the painfullness of being stung. Just like someone 2 years ago that demanded I should trim up and shape some large

Copyright 1910
by Wallace Nutting

MARLBORO BIRCHES   MITCHELL DOOR—NANTUCKET

THE BEAUTIES OF OLD AGE—CARLISLE

AN ORCHARD BORDER—FRANKLIN COUNTY

trees after I had explained to them that as soon as I got off the ground I became very dizzy, their statement was that I must do their work anyway.

I have bees of my own. I shall not care for the bees that are not my own when I let my own go. Mr. —— has an expert that works for him that he has recommended until now it is Mr. ——. besides there are Mr. —— and —— that claim Honors in Bee Handling. But don't be fooled by anyone that I like to Monkey with the Bees. *I won't do it*. More than that I am not a worshiper of aristocracy patronage in any shape or form, so don't be fooled any more."

LAKES OF MASSACHUSETTS

THE largest bodies of fresh water in Massachusetts being reservations, boating in a general way is debarred on them. The lake with the long name briefly called Webster Pond has a contour of wonderful variety and using Webster as a base one may spend a number of interesting days in cruising. The lake's cottage life is attractive partly because there is not very much of it. The group of lakes about Lakeville, south of Middleboro, is very extensive. Long Pond, Assawomsett Pond, Great and Little Quittacas Ponds and Pocksha Pond are all situated about a rough quadrilateral. Some of the islands are sufficiently high to be attractive as residences. An amusing effort has been made to account for the mildness of the winters in this region by the large bodies of fresh water. We would think that when a strong northeast gale was blowing over these ice sheets the fresh water would not temper the wind to the shorn lamb. There is, of course, a cooling of the air in the summer quite noticeable when the breezes come from the waters. These extensive stretches may be mentioned in connection with the entire series of ponds about Plymouth and the Cape. More and more they will become an important esthetic feature.

Among the hundreds of ponds in the state, in which particular it is only surpassed by Maine of the New England states, perhaps the reservoir between Berkshire Village and Cheshire reflecting as it does the higher peaks of the Berkshire Hills is most picturesque of all. It may be circuited by a highway whence it is always in view; and its great length in proportion to its width very much increases its beauty. North Mountain on one side of it at Dalton is 2220 feet high and on the other side Savage Hill is 2000 feet in elevation. Various other peaks form a sky outline as they rise one behind another, of wonderful beauty. Indeed, Cheshire is an important esthetic center, although perhaps a little north of the fashionable district. We know no village in the state so close to lofty mountains with the possible exception of North Adams. But all the way from Cheshire to North Adams and Williamstown the stream in this deep valley affords a multitude of fine prospects.

The Berkshires are blessed with various little mountain lakes some of them of striking beauty. Running into Tyringham from Lee one finds Goose Pond, Upper Goose Pond and Green Water Pond all nestled among lofty hills and situated so as to summon every romantic instinct. Almost the same might be said of the ponds in Becket. Pontoosuc and Onota Lakes in Lanesboro and Pittsfield are very well known but lack the near and lofty effect of the hills. Worcester and Leicester are environed with ponds, Groton has its fair share as have also Westminster and Ashburnham. In fact the fine sites for homes on lookouts about the large and small bodies of water in the state are numerous enough to satisfy everyone and they are by no means all preëmpted. With the modern tendency to concentrate manufacturing these little lakes will be exempt from unsightly features and so far as their power is utilized its use will not mar their beauty.

One may almost say that a country residence is not perfect unless it is within vision of a body of water. That water need not be extensive but if small it should be close at hand. Nothing whatever can take the place of water charm. Its mirror calm, its gently wrinkled surface, changing with infinite variety, gives back to us a succession of pictures now dreamy, now fantastic, now weird and witchlike. What stillness is so emphatic as

HONEYMOON DRIVE—FRANKLIN COUNTY

BLOSSOMS THAT MEET—SHEFFIELD

GARDEN SAMOSET INN — PLYMOUTH

A NASHUA REACH

that of a body of water when absolutely unbroken by a breath? What so fully can dignify and distinguish a landscape as the running margin of a little lake, here graced by great elms, there by drooping birches, beyond by clumps of gorgeous maples or the giant and tortuous limbs of a great oak that have held themselves above the beckoning waters perhaps for centuries.

If Americans are ever to take their birthright to enjoy the beautiful they cannot better begin than by studying the grace of that line where turf and water meet.

ANCIENT HOUSES

ASIDE from general mention in this volume of early dwellings it will, perhaps, be a boon to the general reader to have some critical estimates of the best ancient houses in the state.

There is in Wrentham an ancient dwelling which has never been restored or sought so far as we know for that purpose. It was built in the seventeenth century and the oldest part still has wooden latches and the raised sill over which one must step. Its back door lintel is cut in the great chimney girt to give head room. One may express the hope that a sufficient number of persons of taste for restoring such houses will, in the process of time, gradually acquire and preserve them all, an object so laudably sought by the effective and extensive efforts of the New England Society for the Preservation of Antiquities.

There are some houses Gloucester way, in private hands, which have an overhang on the side and there are two such houses in Saugus. These go with the Paul Revere House in Boston.

The Quincy homestead in the city of that name is a very large and beautifully located dwelling which has an increased interest to us because it is composed of additions made at different periods. The oldest portion places it amongst the earliest in the country and while the kitchen fireplace is wrongly restored being made too small, a defect presumably to be remedied, one must always allow for something of this kind. In fact so rapid has been the increase in knowledge on such subjects and so seldom has anyone had at once the patience, the means and the enthusiasm that we may say that we know of no dwelling restored absolutely as it ought to be and completed. In some cases the errors are not extensive. In other cases work is in process.

The Quincy homestead shows a fascinating development in one of the front rooms where the great panels about the fireplace are swung out to show the ancient simpler forms. Either as it is or as it was the fireplace is excellent. One sees here the beautifully beaded clapboards and many other features within and without which lead one to return often.

In the same town the Adams houses though notable historically and very old are extremely simple and have not yet been fully brought back to their original state. Around one of them there is a marvelously good piece of stone wall and ancient fence which does more to give the original feeling of an old country house than any other process whatever.

The Fairbanks house, casually mentioned before, has some features not found elsewhere. A very important detail is the framing of the interior doors which may exist elsewhere but we have never seen it. The very instability of the foundation of this dwelling gave its roof line the remarkable picturesqueness, such as we see nowhere else. This house is readily seen on the Boston and Providence route.

It would be a matter for a huge volume to mention in detail the merits and romance of all, even of the seventeenth century houses. But the Manning house in Billerica, a private dwelling, is most attractive.

In Salem, the House of the Seven Gables is perhaps better known than any other New England restoration. Its sharp roof lines with their fascinating variety are fitted to enthrall all old house lovers. In Concord the Old Manse is unfortunately not shown. Its setting and situation by the battlefield make it unique.

We show on page eighty-eight a house at East Haverhill which in its

A BERKSHIRE POOL—PITTSFIELD

A LENOX ROAD

IN WEST PITTSFIELD

rooms has sheathed panelling of wonderful mellow yellow of old pine never painted. There are numerous features connected with this dwelling of importance to antiquarians and it is furthermore picturesque. It lies also in a fair country. The drives from Rock Bridge are beautiful though narrow, and other quaint cottages may be detected here and there by those who are given to searching them out.

Very few dwellings in the Connecticut valley outside of those at Deerfield have been preserved from the earliest period. The growth of the valley cities has marked old house destruction. We have elsewhere mentioned many early dwellings.

A late house about the beginning of the nineteenth century is seen on the top of the hill in Brookfield, — the Chapin place. It is interesting from its extremely ornate door showing the last flamboyant development of the elliptical window over the door, its side lights and other features of fenestration.

Pictures of doorways have become very well known as souvenirs and we, therefore, confine ourselves mostly to the quainter and older examples. Anyone, however, who is at all taken with such studies could easily spend several seasons in studying the outlines of the eighteenth century houses in Massachusetts. There are probably more of them of a good character than in any other state, though the somewhat quainter dwellings are perhaps more numerous in Connecticut and are to be treated later on.

We have never tallied the lists of the historical societies in Massachusetts which maintain old dwellings as headquarters. It is, however, a very long list. A delightful month, at least, might be spent exclusively on the visitation of such dwellings. None of them are lacking some important features; some of them are of supreme importance and interest, and taken as a whole, the study of them undertaken in a broad and thorough way will initiate any pilgrim from the West into most of the best of history, romance, architecture and antiquities of earliest America.

We do not forget Virginia, but the greater part of the stately dwellings there is of a period rather later than those we have dwelt upon here.

ENTRANCE TO WAYSIDE INN

DIFFERENCES IN TASTE

THE versatility of human nature is one of its most pleasing aspects, especially when considered in reference to the location and the sort of homes that people chose.

A gentleman of much culture made the remark that his family preferred a house where they could speak across to the back door of their neighbors. This was at least human and gregarious, however much it differs from the Englishman's house-castle idea. The gentleman quoted was frank. Perhaps a great many others have a sly liking for this same sort of a dwelling. At least, a great many people dwell in such conditions and we must believe that what people do continuously they do by preference, not always but generally.

BROOKFIELD BLOSSOMS

THE FAIRBANKS HOMESTEAD — DEDHAM

THE POOL'S CORNER

LEOMINSTER COTTAGE

We notice also that many dwellings are erected on land so low that water lies in their cellars, although within a stone's throw there is higher land. It would be a fascinating study to trace the stream loving habit back to the beginnings of history. We remember that various English cathedrals are built on bogs by the side of streams. That at Winchester, we remember, fell once and would have fallen again for this reason had it not been buttressed with great care.

The water way being the original road the dwelling was close to the bank partly from convenience and partly from the love of human association. A study of old London indicates that much of its present ground was once under water and the huts by the river were, of course, its beginning.

We have in Boston, the metropolis of our state, a great area containing the fashionable district which was once under water.

An odd shift of fashion, probably inaugurated by men of historic imagination, has caused a return to Beacon Hill which forty years ago had degenerated to a region of cheap boarding houses and often of negro habitation, though its dwellings were architectually fine. Of course, Beacon Hill was always as desirable as it is now. It is very near the State House and in fact the nearest dwelling house district in the city to the great centers of banking and trade. It required strength of mind to bring about the present desirable state of affairs. But whatever induced people to leave quarters so nearly ideal if anything in a city can be ideal? How much taste influences fashion is a nice question. In this case once the ball was set rolling everything was in favor of the return to this neighborhood. It is true that the Fenway district in Boston has charms if one is near some of its redeemed waterways. But we are reminded that just now one of our friends was warned out of an apartment in the Fenway district in order that the sagging foundation might be reinforced.

Everywhere men have first collected for commercial reasons by the banks of streams. Though in the feudal era the tops of hills were chosen as citadels, the town has been on the low lands and it is in the low lands that the best soils for cultivation lie. It is probable that the habit of living on low land is so thoroughly ingrained in human nature through a myriad of generations of evolution that it will never be eradicated. Wherever we journey we find the great aggregations of population are in the valley.

In our book on Vermont we have taken up quite thoroughly the motives that induced country settlements on hills in portions of New England.

But the matter of taste in the location of a dwelling is we fear, or should we say we hope, not so much one of deliberate choice as a fortuitous occurrence. On first reaching a town with the purpose of settlement a family is most likely to take up what they think of as temporary quarters and these quarters are near the center. Habit does the rest. We would gladly believe that most human dwellings as we see them are not deliberately chosen but are considered as make-shifts. Whether they are so considered or not we can give them no other name. Probably the most stinging disgrace in America today is the shoddy character of its dwellings. Yet these dwellings cost infinitely more than in any other region on earth, but the French and for the most part the English and other civilized peoples build their dwellings to last.

Apart from the matter of dwellings the divergence of human tastes in the matter of recreation is amusing. What would make a perfect summer for one would be very nearly perfect torture for another. We revert in the summer to our primeval tastes and perhaps the majority of men in their love for fishing and hunting merely prove that the occupations of their ancestors still call them. Perhaps it is only a perch or a squirrel that is brought back but fine air and exercise and an opportunity to be poetic and romantic as well as esthetic has been afforded. Perhaps it would be better not to inquire too particularly how far advantage is taken of these opportunities. It is none of our business, most would say, what they are thinking about or whether they are thinking at all. They are resting from thinking and reverting to a dreamy past. They are allowing their ragged nerves to knit again by sheer neglect. We have friends

A CROSS COUNTRY ROAD—FRANKLIN COUNTY

MANY HAPPY RETURNS—HARVARD

BERKSHIRE VILLAGE BEECHES

THE MISSION DOOR—STOCKBRIDGE

who spend their summers hunting prehistoric Indian graves. Others will search through ten states for a butterfly. Why not? Before we condemn the childishness of pleasures we should remember that the more idle the pleasure the more wise it may be. If men do not know what amuses them how can we tell them? Of course our own pleasures are the only wise ones. But in all seriousness those pleasures which open some avenue of the natural world are certainly highly rational and happily to most are interesting. We are still of the opinion that to a great majority there are better things than spending one's summer shuffling cards.

It is said to be a time of faddists. Every human frame must have something taken out of it or a gland put into it. Every school, whatever the multiplicity of its curricula, should according to some learned men take on one or two more branches. Even old Jonathan Edwards preached a sermon on the sin of failing to sing in meeting whether one could sing or not. If he converted everyone to the effort of trying could any sensitive person have borne it? Every great man is a little of a fool, and if he is a very great man he is in some particulars also a great fool. It is only mediocre people who never do anything silly.

We are a little weary of those persons who test everything by sound common sense or tradition or any other standard except decency. It is by the faddist and the extremist that various avenues of human experiment have been followed out. Thus the sum of human knowledge is increased and if some follow a blind alley they may at least report the fact. The learned man whose strange occupations are such a wonder to the farmer is not so big a fool as he seems. He is simply thinking in one direction while the farmer thinks in a direction equally important for the progress of humanity.

Just now we are told there is an epidemic of Egyptian styles with their harsh and lean angles and semi-barbaric uncouthness against which all mouths are supposed to be closed because these things showed the climax of Egyptian art. We object to the fallacy that art is not to be challenged. No permanent harm can come of uncouth tastes. They are like the

A QUINCY DOOR

measles and must have their run.   Nations must get them out of their systems.

As to Massachusetts Beautiful the lack of good taste or its confinement to a few objects or localities may hinder the spread of estheticism till, on a returning tide, beauty claims its own everywhere.

Of course, speaking broadly, every landscape can be made charming. There is one glory of the mountain and another of the valley.   There is a splendor of the seashore and a rapture in a nook of the hills.   There is a convincing bible in the sky and a philosophy in the forest.   We dwell

CRESS BROOK ROAD — NORFOLK

A HOME OVER THE ROAD — MIDDLESEX

THE LITTLE COVE — BURLINGTON

ROWLEY MARSHES

in a favored land where all tastes may find food and may embody themselves measurably as they will.

We should only remember in practice that there need be no plague spots of unsightliness anywhere; that poverty does not necessarily mean dirt or baldness; that the simple life gains as much as it loses and perhaps many fold more; that the lavish output of wealth develops a state in certain ways that eventually may turn to good.

We set our faces toward the abolition of smoke and dust. We hope for a universal insistence on roadside decency and an effort to make the world attractive. We have seen many portents of failure but we see a multitude more of prophetic success.

Even a race so marked by folly as our own must learn at length that civilization need not be ugly nor politics base.

THE RIVER CHARLES

SOMETHING has been written a long time since of the River Charles. We think also that a canoe trip over the length of the stream has been reported. The river with its newly pent in banks between Boston and Cambridge is an important and attractive feature. As one ascends it leaving Brookline on the left and Cambridge on the right he passes then between Watertown and Newton under occasional bridges.

The river is beautiful to a degree in its irregular shores below Riverside between Weston and Newton and again, between Wellesley and Newton, Echo Bridge has long been a popular point to visit.

The stretches between Needham and Dedham show occasional bold rock banks and sometimes a marsh. The course of the river is exceedingly tortuous, and there is an old cut-off in Dedham which constitutes a large island nearly a mile in its greatest length.

The region of Charles River Village between Needham and Dover is also good. There are considerable marshes between Dover and Wellesley.

The upper reaches from Dover to the source are less well known but are more beautiful than the region below. Between Sherborn and Medfield and particularly in Millis there are fine birches and elms and very many points where an artist, it would seem, should make a canvas of wonderful beauty.

This volume shows several views of the stream in Millis and Needham. An old dam at Rockville throws the water back for some miles and various pasture knolls open vistas which in England would be claimed as advantageous locations for country seats. Through Medway and West Medway this stream is rapidly coming to the various brooks which form its source in Holliston, Milford, Bellingham and Franklin. Dover in recent years and now Millis and to some extent Medfield and Medway, have come to be sought as the locations of good country homes. It will be a labor of love on the part of those who come to find the beauties of the Charles and to make them better known. Massachusetts, aside from the Merrimac and the Connecticut, neither of which she can claim as wholly or even principally her own, must depend upon the beauties of the Charles as her principal waterway attraction with the possible exception of the Housatonic, which also is not wholly within her borders.

We recall, in particular, certain points in Millis near Rockville where the river is unsurpassed as a decorative landscape feature, reached as it is by soft rolling hills. It is up this stream that the first and second generations of the settlers came by boat and established their homes well before the end of the seventeenth century. Some of the dwellings of that period still remain. The landscape has that air of long occupation and homelikeness that we see in England. The gently sloping meadows and the old stone bridges give an air of continuity and calm. It would be easily possible to provide a whole volume of illustrations, all beautiful, of this river and its attractive little tributaries, coming down from Walpole, Norfolk and Wrentham.

That portion of the stream in Cambridge upon which Longfellow looked and that he loved so much is to be preserved as a memorial of that

WESTFIELD WATER

DECKED AS A BRIDE—FRANKLIN COUNTY

THE SHORT HOUSE—NEWBURY

dear spirit. We do not know how much he knew of the river near its source, but ever it is that portion of any stream where the banks are near enough together to be acquainted and where they may talk across as it were that one feels the finest attraction. There is an intimacy and a sense of home waters in the vicinity of a little river.

We have sometimes considered the joyful task of illustrating this stream very fully so as to show a typical instance to our Western friends of the abounding esthetic features of New England. One might embark, for instance, on the Mississippi at the southern point of Minnesota and see merely a dull monotony of shore for thousands of miles. Mud, snags and featureless sameness, depite a few bluffs of even outline, would mark his progress to the very gulf. It is something to live in a country where at every bend of the stream there is a fresh attraction and inspiration for poet and painter and home maker and a call to that in us which leads out the more mellow, winning, reflective phases of character.

CHANGING OWNERSHIP OF FARMS

ON many of the roads out of Boston, especially south and southwest, one sometimes sees stately old dwellings with pigs running about the door, and every evidence of decline. This decline, however, relates merely to the farm buildings. The farm itself has been sold to immigrants who are thinking exclusively of the commercial side. They are keeping up the fertility of the acres or restoring them but they have no appreciation for the beautiful. We hear indignation expressed about this state of affairs but if the owners died, or living, had not the pride or energy to keep up their places someone must own them. Certainly unless a critic himself has redeemed some such country place his mouth is stopped.

This changing condition of ownership is so general, especially in eastern Massachusetts, that we would say the majority of the old families have

THE ELEAZER ARNOLD HOUSE

left their places. Either they lie in the churchyard or have gone to town
or to the West. There are districts where a generally shabby condition
continues on long stretches of road. Where, as in the case of Millis,
Dover and other towns, land values become high, there is likely to be a
shifting back of many of these old places into the hands of Americans who
are able to restore them to their pristine attractions. But it is wonderful
how the immigrant will stick in some instances even when his land values
become very high, and there are spots which are likely to be eyesores for
a long time until his children or children's children shall catch the better
American spirit of improvement. We are free to say that the native
American had allowed the process of deterioration to begin, but he drew
a line at pigs on the porch.

It will be feasible for a long time for many who are totally blind to the

A PLYMOUTH GARDEN HOUSE

A CORNER OF PLEASANT BAY

PROVINCETOWN HOLLYHOCKS

A DENNIS LILY POOL

esthetic to retain extensive acreage because nearness to a great city will give high values to the land for market gardening. We remember an instance where a malodorous garden of this sort extended to the very windows of a wonderful old mansion. A young scion of the family married and returned to the house and purchased back enough of the family acres to free him of the offensive intrusion.

So far as Italians are buying these lands there is hope that their artistic strain may crop out and that they will seek for beauty about their homesteads. But however much we may admire the Italian art temperament, there is no nation consisting to any large extent of artists. It would be invidious to mention some of the other nationalities that have purchased old Massachusetts homesteads. One or two nationalities very thrifty, but devoted to the compost heap and accustomed in the old world to pile it near their front doors, may take long to get better ideas. The conservatism of some foreign farmers is only equalled by some of our own.

We remember instances where farms in the center or western part of the state have been purchased by the Hebrews and become centers around which gather innumerable decrepit automobiles or carts or rubbish until we conclude that a cyclone must have swept through. The Hebrew begins by cultivating the soil ostensibly, but he invariably ends by being a cattle trader or a trader in something, and it is very seldom that one sees him striking his hoe into the soil.

Perhaps we ought to be glad that anybody wants our country acres. We are in a state of flux at present and the future of farms fifty years hence will be very different. The specializing process will have proceeded farther and there will be more attention to neatness and, indeed, to beauty on the part of those who are now just getting their start.

We may forget that an old farm is bought under a heavy mortgage and that the buyers are busily engaged in clearing off the mortgage. Some Americans would buy and borrow on a mortgage to improve the buildings. The foreign buyer is wiser. He wishes to own his acres and to proceed on a safer line.

Meantime the state must suffer the dilapidation incident to poverty or lack of taste. The influence of example, however, is universal and an attractive farm place never exists long without imitators. We have noticed many instances where a door head or a form of gable was copied for miles around. This imitative spirit will come in good stead as time goes on and the daughters of aliens become thoroughly American and will desire homes as well kept as their neighbors.

The writer has a great respect for the diligence and capacity of most of the immigrant buyers of eastern farms. They at least look the world frankly in the face and expect to get their living out of the soil. In this they are succeeding far more often than the American farmer of the old stock.

We remember seeing a great many years ago a cartoon showing the forebears of the Knickerbocker families disembarking from a Dutch ship at Manhattan. Certainly as to cleanliness and education and property they had very little to recommend them. The glamour of tradition happily cast about our ancestors some attractive traits which they may not have possessed. At least they knew how to dig and they came here to dig and they are now well entrenched. We are very hopeful of improved country sides in Massachusetts into whosesoever hands they may now have fallen.

THE NASHUA RIVER

THE Nashua River in its Massachusetts course passes through some of the most beautiful intervale towns anywhere to be found. Taking its rise in the hills of Worcester county and gathering to the great Clinton reservoir, it flows through Lancaster in a course of exquisite beauty amidst splendid trees. It meets at South Lancaster the North Nashua River and moves on into Harvard. A branch in that town called Still River, on a perfectly level plain, is full of fascination from its fine foliage banks.

THE BEST OF THE BIRCHES—LENOX-STOCKBRIDGE

HOUSATONIC CURVES

MOUNTING THE MOHAWK TRAIL

At Shirley it meanders by the base of fine hills and flowing, in the main, nearly north, passes through Groton with many a curve of beauty. Then at Pepperell, although the river has passed its youth, it has not lost its beauty. We lose it to New Hampshire among the Nissitissit Hills. If one is looking for splendid trees and fine meadows, on a stream, we would say he should seek no farther than the valley of the Nashua. The soil in the bottom lands of this stream seems to be perfectly adapted for great tree growths. The elm, in particular, seems to reach a climax of super-abundant life in this neighborhood, and our pictures of The Seven Bridge Road and of The Nashua Asleep, and other scenes along the stream, record certain of its aspects.

If one were transported blindfold to Lancaster or Harvard he might almost mistake his surroundings for an old world country, since there is such a number of culture features, which have taken advantage of the waters.

OTHER STREAMS

THE western branch of the Westfield River as one comes down from the heights of the Berkshires in Washington between Middlefield and Becket to Chester, and meeting there with Walker Brook, and going on through Chester to Westfield, by the Jacob's Ladder trail, shows a great deal of variety in its course. In its upper waters it is a rapidly rushing torrent, with here and there a lucid interval, by a mill dam or a small meadow. By the time it reaches Westfield, however, it becomes more sedate, mature with broadening and ripening charms.

The Sudbury and the Assabet, meeting to form the Concord, each has many alluring curves with finely draped foliage banks.

It is, however, the smaller streams feeding these rivers that provide the more cosey and hidden nooks and banks of beauty.

In the northwest of the state the Hoosic River, while marred by lines

A WEYMOUTH HOMESTEAD

of railways, here and there escapes contamination, and wanders to a silent and secluded shrine, where it communes with the grasses and woodlands. It moves between noble hills which afford some of the most beautiful scenes in Massachusetts.

THE OLD STAGE DRIVER

THIS picturesque figure is lost to us, but in his day he was an institution not so reserved and haughty as his great-coated English cousin. The Yankee stage driver descended to common things and did not hold himself above the upper middle class!   In the informal American life he could often descend to joke with his passengers.   Asked what the fare was he might reply, " Wal, I charge homely girls seventy-five cents, but girls as good lookin' as you are ought not to pay over half a dollar."

A FERN PATH—PITTSFIELD

BELCHERTOWN MEADOWS

A LINKS POOL — NORTH ADAMS

A BERKSHIRE MEADOW — PITTSFIELD

He was a resourceful character, he knew everybody, did errands for the housewives along the route, and was a connecting link for the neighborhood. We will not say that he did not relish imparting the news. In fact, he was somewhat of an artist in this matter, and could, on occasion, throw in a touch of embellishment which gave a certain finish and interest to his tale. As his vehicle was too jolty to permit reading, he became the natural partner in conversations on the long road, and while he would not often grudgingly admit the things he knew, he did not hesitate to take for granted, to some degree, things that he did not know.

He was an intense local patriot. There was no country as good as this through which he drove, and no town equal to that in which he was at present. To be sure the roads could be better, but he believed in fighting it out on that line. He grew old in his service, and his whimsies came to be understood by dwellers on his route. Happily, however, there were enough strangers, especially in the summer, to laugh afresh at his old saws and modern instances. In fact, if a summer guest came to abide in the hill town, it was necessary to run the gauntlet of the stage driver's questions. He sought indirectly, and then if his quest did not bring the desired information, by the most direct methods, the origin, age, family connections, profession, financial standing and any other unconsidered trifles relating to the traveler. It was a kind of moral obligation, an eleventh commandment so to speak, which touched his professional pride, to say that he was " posted " as to the new comer at Taylor's boarding house.

We began to make pictures while he was still on his route. He eyed with much curiosity the square boxes connected with the picture processes. The tripod might have been a surveyor's. " Makin' pictures? What do you do with them? Would anybody want a picture of that brook? Well, the fools ain't all dead yet. How long are you goin' to stay? How much can you git for them? Yer don't say! What will you charge to make a picture of my pair? "

It was then our turn. " Do you think your pair are an art subject? " " Wal, I don't know about that, but they have hauled a great many big men, some of them bigger than you be, I reckon."

Another driver was a good deal bothered to make us out. Finally he was in such obvious distress that we volunteered the information that we got our living largely out of apple trees. " Oh," said he, " You are in the nursery business." " No." He looked a little thrown off but came back with the reply, " Oh yes, I see, you buy apples." " No." " Look here, you ain't one of them men that buy up old orchards to make tool handles, are ye? " " No." The poor fellow was at the end of his invention and relapsed into a distressed silence. It was too bad to keep him in suspense further, so we informed him that our business in the apple trees had to do with the blossoms. This completely passed the realm of his experience, and it took him all summer to get over it. Pictures of blossoms! Wal, they are kind of pretty now you come to think of it. Where do the pictures go? Often to the South and West where people think they are peach blooms, but some people never believe it when we tell them they are apple blossoms. They say no apple tree ever grew as large as that. " Huh! You tell them Colorado fellows to come up here to the old Orcutt place, and I will show 'em apple tree trunks three foot through."

AUNT MARY'S

WE are off for a little country village in an intervale between the higher hills. We must be there professionally for some months and are recommended to Aunt Mary's. As the deacon said in the prayer meeting, we have passed through seens and unseens, in the way of boarding houses, and we received with some skepticism the recommendations about Aunt Mary's.

We are met by a little woman in black. She is made even smaller by stooped shoulders. Her eyes, however, are full of sparkling intelligence

BLACK AND WHITE—SWAMPSCOTT

DOWN THE ORCHARD ROAD—NEAR MONSON

BLOSSOM ARCH—LITTLETON

BIRCH WRAITHS—NORTHFIELD

and kindliness. She shows us to a great square chamber as neat as the most fastidious could wish. It is, in fact, as neat as a dear old maid can make it. There are four windows, there is a quaint old fireplace, there are old steel engravings and old time prints. The paper is covered with little posies, and the furniture, happily, was made before the worst period when men, seeking after originality, produced the most ugly shapes imaginable.

Left to ourselves we sit by a window on the side of the house and peer out into the garden and the orchard, an advance guard of which stands sociably near. Ah, yes, he reaches out an arm with a large cluster of August fruit, taking on fine colors in the splashes of sunlight that shoot through the waving bough. We advance a hand to meet this friendly overture and can actually touch the ripening fruit. We find out later from Aunt Mary that if we are here a month it will be ripe for us to pluck, and that is the special perquisite of the occupants of that room. There is another branch above us arching the window, and when the breeze takes the bough a gentle and friendly brushing against the clapboards occurs.

We are the first of Aunt Mary's boarders for the season. She has a fine spirited girl who goes to school at the academy, and helps Aunt Mary at table. How delectable was that picked-up chicken! Did ever a dish of apple dowdy go to the spot like that? And the blueberry muffins are beyond praise. We dream of them yet.

As boarders come, now one, now another, from the great city we find them all a picked company, who are there because they love Aunt Mary and her ways and works. It appears later that she was induced to part with her little old wood stove and get a modern range, but in a few days out it went and back came the companion of her youth, whose ways she knew.

Of course, a company like this must go rowing on the river one day, and down to the pond another day. Two or three young men make up a party to climb the heights and remain over night. A maiden of rather mature charms, or at least what she would have thought to be charms, has

ON HAMILTON-WENHAM ROAD

from year to year set her cap for the new bachelor boarders but so far in vain. Hope, however, springs eternal in the human breast. She can hardly understand how any one should prefer to tramp along the brooks after trout, rather than read with her in the afternoons from the romances of Wilkie Collins. Aunt Mary assumes a motherly direction over all her charges. They are not merely boarders. They are her own family, and she privately warns them of the snares set. The two high school girls are her special anxiety lest any cynical city youth should make an impression upon them. The two school teachers, however, who have imbibed modern notions, Aunt Mary feels are old enough to take care of themselves, and her sympathies are on the side of the bachelors in that case.

It is an interesting little world. A good boarding house is the next thing to a home. Sweet airs blow through. If ever an odor is noticed

THE TALL PINES OF LENOX

WHITE CLUSTERS—LENOX

WHITE STUDDED CURVES—LENOX

from the kitchen it is of that delectable sort just sufficient to whet our appetites for the coming feast.

The old parlor with its hair cloth sofa, is the room where culprits or suspects meet Aunt Mary; also, if they need a confidant, they may depend upon her. Sitting with her on the sofa we are aware of her tender concern, her unshaken righteousness and her wisdom. It is safe to tell Aunt Mary what is in your mind. Not only so, but it is not safe to do anything else. From many a danger she frees us, and causes us to walk in the way of the just — if she can.

Aunt Mary could live the year around, outside of the summer time, a welcome guest in town, with the various persons whom she has cared for at her old homestead. No one ever forgets her nor does she forget any. All who ever enter her doors become her correspondents, and it is not well for them if they allow too long an interval to elapse without suggestions from her wisdom.

She is getting very old now and a little more stooped. Her fine black hair one no longer finds, but a cap covers the few stray gray locks. Blessed be the day that we found Aunt Mary's. Like the Being whom she worships, she is good to all and her tender mercies are over all her works. For so little a woman what a heart she has! The sorrows and joys of multitudes are shared there. The secret griefs, woes and even sins of many are there buried. She is a second mother to many a man now himself getting gray. She is better than her dear old home and its orchard; better than her fair village. She is really the heart of life. She inherits the best of everything and is the fountain of good.

We dread for ourselves but hope for her the word that she is no longer with us. She will give up her cares unwillingly or would do so, did she not feel sure that a kind Over-soul will give her other responsibilities. For Aunt Mary would be miserable without much to do and many to love. One begins by bargaining with her for board, and one ends by wishing he could give her more than money. That person is a cheat who doesn't share with Aunt Mary the best of his thoughts and the truest of his affections.

ON THE CONCORD-ACTON ROAD

BUYING AN OLD FARM

WE actually did buy an old farm and the experiences related below are a few of those that came to us.

One is not long in possession of an old country place before suggestions begin to come in from the neighbors of what to do with it. A lady suggested that we take out the big old chimney and put in a smaller one, as it would give more room, and "lots of people were having their houses fixed that way." As we had purchased the house largely because it had a fine old stone chimney the advice came as a shock. The additional room was not needed. The house was of two stories, and had a quaint entry with the stairs running up on the front face of the chimney. It is not a modern stair, indeed, but we are convinced from large experience that the

AS IT WAS IN 1700—BILLERICA

ONOTA LAKE—PITTSFIELD

A PEMBROKE GARDEN

A BERKSHIRE FLUME

way to ruin any house is to try to make it a different style than it was in-tended. A house should be restored according to its period, or let severely alone.

All that had saved this old chimney in the past, when an L was built, was the insistence of the aged mother that the chimney be left as an " anchor." So far as we can learn the thought was that a huge old chim-ney prevented the possibility of wreckage by wind storm. We see many a solid ancient chimney standing after the dwelling of which it formed the core has gone.

On our first Sunday at church we found a preacher whose weekday business was the sale of spectacles. It was appropriate enough. He tried to get the people to see clearly the truth of the spirit on Sundays. He was paid five dollars and drove into town and out again. A cobweb was sus-pended from the preacher's desk and a window was full of hornets. There was a suggestion of the wiles of sin and the snares set for souls in the cobweb, and the hornets might have answered as an illustration, but the sermon had been prepared beforehand, — a long time!

We were asked if we sang, and were handed the hymn book opened at the Doxology. The elderly dame who did this courtesy was informed that we had been officers in a church. " Oh, well," said she, " I suppose you know the Doxology. I do."

On investigating a church fund for the support of preaching it appears that an endowment had been furnishing the five dollars a week aforesaid, on condition that four sermons a year be preached on Foreordination. No collection was taken. Probably the endowment has demoralized the en-tire neighborhood. A people who do not carry their own church have no religion worth speaking about.

In trying to bring the old house back to its original condition we tear down a useless partition. We have been saying that it is a pre-Revolu-tionary house. As the debris between the plaster drops, out comes a beautiful skeleton. " Ah," says the housewife, " a pre-Revolutionary rat! "

The old tall clock looks well but is somewhat uncertain in its movements. Happily we hit upon a way of setting it without asking any questions. After inquiring the time for some days, we find that the carpenter sneezes regularly at 1:20 P.M. We throw this out as a suggestion. Perhaps it may not be as reliable as the Washington Observatory, but we never know it to fail.

The previous owner had a highly decorated stove instead of a fireplace. He was in the habit of placing his feet on the fender, wrapping himself in a bed quilt and, seated in a Boston rocker, spending the night there. He said it saved the trouble of undressing and dressing. We are learning fast.

The night that the cows we had purchased come home finds us in a dilemma. We have cows but no milk pail. We are obliged to milk in a tin dipper. It takes one member of the party to hold the dipper and another to do the milking. We hear of another city farmer who had a like experience, and also forgot his milk pans.

The question of country help enlivens but does not always delight us. Our maid of all work we find one day has been short of a belt, and has discovered in the waste basket an old typewriter ribbon wherewith she has girded herself. The color on the shirt waist is quite effective.

Our first churning is enlivening. We stir the cream. The cream is too cold and we bring it to the stove. The husband, the wife, the niece and a hired man assist by turns. But these come in the form of relays or advisers. At first one person is supposed to be enough. We discover at last that the cream is now too warm, and it is removed to sulk for a day in the distant pantry. Four churners, four hours. When the battle is over the entire pantry is streaked with spatters of cream but the butter has come. Our niece has pearls of cream beautifully distributed in her hair.

There is a cat that comes with the farm. She is somewhat of an institution, and is commended affectionately to our care. Her upkeep is less than that of an ordinary cat because she lacks a tail. In process of time there is an addition to the family and after a few months we smile to find

LAKE   CHAUGGOGGAGOGMANCHAUGGAGOGCHABUNAGUNGAMAUG

HAPPY VALLEY ROAD—BUCKLAND

TRAILSIDE BLOOMS—ERVING

ourselves sitting about the fireplace one evening with a cat or a kitten on the lap of every member of the family. A truly domestic scene.

When the old house is restored to its original condition so far as we can do so, it is time to consider the grounds. A fine clump of locusts borders one corner of the lot; several pines at another angle shield us from the down valley winds. Then comes a row of maples and outside the lot, bordering the street, a row of elms. There is a definite slope in all directions to the brook, which is rather bushy and inclined to be swampy, but it is so far below the house that we find it feasible to throw a dam across a narrow glen, and provide ourselves with a mere. Please note this word. No man going into the country and building a dam forms a pond thereby. It is always a mere or a lake or lakelet or a pool or something of that kind. And also, a city man should not refer to his farm but to his country estate. Has it not gate posts? Is there not a drive nearly a hundred feet long? And has it not a name?

From time immemorial the district has been called Poverty. Perhaps the name is prophetic. We try out several names. One is Leaky Gables. Its fits but is a trifle personal. A friend of ours suggests the name Weedy-lawn. If we spend as much energy in devising the rotation of crops as we do in the naming of that place the exchequer will balance better. The neighbors call it Robert's Folly. Rambling Roofs might have done, but, if you love alliteration, Mossy Mound or Locust Lodge would not be so bad.

The exterior of our house we find to be merely clapboarded on the studding and not boarded at all, an ancient fashion in some parts of the country. For increased warmth and economy we place tar paper outside the clapboards and run laths up and down to hold the paper in place and put another set of clapboards on outside the laths. We secure, thus, a very warm house and the effect is good because the window sash projects sufficiently to permit this treatment. Of course we are sorry to lose the effect of the wide projection.

We point up the old stone chimney, with its cornice. We use white paint on the house. Red would have been better, though a red painted house is warmer in summer. We repair the old wall, that borders the road, and is very effective. An old open shed is closed in and becomes a hen house, and the square formed by this, with a tool and cart shed, and a barn, is put in decent order and painted red.

The farm land is much of a puzzle. There is plenty of wood in the decayed trees by the roadsides and in the old orchards. We set out a considerable orchard. In the spring many of the trees have been banded by mice and others have disappeared. The orchard is over the hill where we can not see what is happening, but it is obvious that others also wish to go into orcharding.

The slopes, here and there, of the pasture, are decorated with fine spindling cedars like those one sees in Italy. We are so unwise as to remove a portion of these, with the idea of clearing up the pastures. We lose more than we gain.

Cabbages appeal very strongly to the new farmer. It is easy to see that at three cents a pound, one hundred thousand will bring in a sufficient income. We go in for cabbages. In the autumn we sell them for fifty cents a barrel, we paying for the barrels and the freight and the gathering. The total loss is not more than a couple of thousand dollars. Nevertheless, the lesson is well learned, and it is that the farmer should never confine himself to a single crop, or indeed to two. In the long run, if he has a variety of crops, one will bring a good price if another sells low. We are helped out a little by potatoes, which are fine, large and productive, and bring a round figure.

The woodlot supplies fence posts for sale and furnishes a fund large enough to pay the taxes.

The garden is our delight. It is highly successful.

Our conclusion, after seven years, is that a farmer must be trained, and that he must himself work constantly in the field. He cannot gain anything on the wages of employees. They all cost more than they produce. At present the little, one man farm, is the only safe one, unless, in a very

A NOOK BESIDE MOHAWK TRAIL

A MASSACHUSETTS ROAD IN MAY—ENFIELD

PITTSFIELD WINDINGS

THE RIVER—NORTH ADAMS

big way, one specializes on blooded stock of the highest strains, or secures, through years of effort and advertising, a special market.

But a farm for one who has been a city dweller does much to take the conceit out of him, and to give him back health.   He sleeps well and inevitably becomes bucolic.

The flings made at the farmer for not reading more, fail to take account of the circumstances.   At the end of a long day he is inevitably drowsy. He must rise early.   His evenings are short, but at that he is as well read as the average mechanic, perhaps.

At least we make our premises alluring to the eye and, when the object of the country sojourn is achieved, it is easy to dispose of our holdings.

We have a dear memory; but it is heartbreaking to leave such a heavenly environment.   The waters are soft and beautiful at twilight.   The tree toads answer one another, and the evening songsters call from the grove. The bleat of the lamb and the deeper toned answer of the mother is borne to us.   The great vase elms are outlined against the evening sky in a vague and protective canopy.   The evening star begins to twinkle over the tall pine.

A sweet, almost sacred, stillness falls.   We are enfolded in the kindly curtain of the night.   The embers glow in the waning light and the dancing shadows liven all the great room with odd figures.   Bobby, the kitten, goes to sleep curled up in a big cap that we have dropped in a chair.   We need little and we have much.   Is there not a book shelf, even a repetition of them, each five feet long?   Is there not good cream rising in the pantry?   There will be blackberries enough to go with it for breakfast. The garden has some good things for us, and today's eggs are in the old wooden tray.   The wood pile is ample and the old apple logs give us abundant heat.   We do not lock the doors.   It is time to put out the cat, wind the tall clock, cover the embers and go up the old winding stairs to the square chamber.

A look before retiring discloses from our windows a world of sweetness and beauty.   There can be nothing better anywhere.   Love, health, com-

COOPER-AUSTIN HOUSE—CAMBRIDGE

fort, beauty, warmth and sleep! The lore of the past to divert our leisure, the joy of battling the winter's storm, the joy of gathering autumn fruit, the joys of the fold and the fireside are all ours. All that we want and more than we need are ours. There are enough good neighbors to keep up our faith in the inherent nobility of human nature. They are kind to one another in times of trouble. Their innocent gossip is diverting. Within a few miles by charming drives we may reach centers of human activity. Whoever wants more than these things should keep away from the country, for his soul must be dull to its beauty and its joy.

TAIL RACE AND BRIDGE—SUDBURY

NEWBURYPORT TURNPIKE

WILLIAMSTOWN WATERWAY

A TREE OF LIFE BEDSPREAD

HOW TO SELECT A FARM PLACE

1st. Do not despise small buildings. It is easy to spend and sometimes one begins too large. A little cottage doubled is far more artistic than a big square house.

2nd. Avoid clay soil for your residence. It is damp most of the year and the cellar is always so. Seek clay soils for at least a portion of your land. Clay is the foundation of agriculture. Soils are divided into clay, clay loam (three-quarters clay, one-quarter sand), loam (half and half), sandy loam (three-quarters sand, one-quarter clay), and sand. Sand is valueless, sandy loam requires much feeding, but is quick and good for a garden. Loam is good crop land. Clay loam is good crop and farm land, but clay is very stiff and hard to handle, though perfect for grass sod that is not often to be turned over, and is the strongest soil in the world.

3rd. Avoid rocky fields. It never pays to clear stones. It takes generations and then they are not cleared. Such fields may be turned into pastures if there is a moderate amount left of easily arable soil. Occasional small stones do no harm, but ledgy fields or fields with numerous small stones are vexing and profitless.

4th. In ledgy or stony ground an orchard may be set, as such soil is often well fitted for fruit and sheep. Sheep may be turned to graze in this pasture if the trees are protected by wires. The orchard should be in sight of the house on account of the sheep as well as the fruit.

5th. Find a country place with possible spring sources to feed the house, by gravity. This is highly desirable, as constant pumping even by machinery is a perpetual nuisance and expense.

6th. Seek first for a farm off the road, approached by its own little side road. Such places are not liked by native country people, and are sold low, whereas the best taste marks such places as altogether more valuable. If an estate effect, seclusion and removal from possible unpleasant bounds, is sought, such a place is worth at least twice as much as one on the main road.

7th. Avoid buildings where the barns are so placed as to interfere with the outlook. If barns or out buildings are very numerous it is far better to remove the poorer ones. There are almost always too many and the upkeep of many buildings is very expensive.

8th. The intimate view is more important than the distant view. If there are good trees, gentle slopes, or a near-by brook, these are the things with which one lives. The distant view is to be desired but is not at all of the first importance, and if an elevation means wind and bareness it is better avoided. The ideal location is a high slope, not too steep, and one that is sufficiently wooded.

9th. Bury your telephone wires or bring them in from the rear. It is almost better not to live in the country if there are to be poles on your road. If electric lighting is not supplied there are modern systems now of great efficiency, and some degree of economy, that are quite satisfactory.

10th. A tractor capable of cutting the old wood around the farm, as well as ploughing and hauling, is now of the first importance, and will save its cost several times over in a short time.

11th. Do not go into any kind of farming that leaves you stranded in the case of failure of help. A farmer can himself feed a number of sheep and young stock, but if he has more than one or two cows his labors become onerous in case farm hands desert him. That is to say, no milk farm should be undertaken, except the farmer is absolutely sure of his men, through long knowledge of them, and an agreement covering a term of years.

12th. Make all arrangements so that you will be as independent as possible of outside connections of men, animals, machines or power.

13th. Farm lands should contain fields, pastures and wood land, whatever else they may lack. Good orchards can seldom be bought. The pasture is important because it affords the most natural, most economical and least troublous method of summer feeding. Many old fields ought never to have been taken out of the pasture. A wood lot is important for the sense of independence it gives, for its esthetic advantage, and also and

A CONCORD WAYSIDE

THE VALLEY OF NORTH ADAMS

A RICHMOND ELM SYMPHONY

THE CONNECTICUT TRAIL — WAYLAND

perhaps principally as an investment.   Almost any good wood lot, if properly bought, will "clear up" more than it cost.   We know of several instances where wood has been sold, so that the farm place then stood the buyer less than nothing.   The wood develops quietly over in the remote corner of the farm and its progress is often unnoticed.   The joy of having a supply of old knotty pieces for the fireplace is great, and costs only the labor.

14th.   Do not bother to drain swampy lands unless the soil is imperatively required.   Coarse grass has its uses, and in a dry season it is often a resource.

15th.   Small fruits carefully attended are a pretty sure source of some profit.   High bush berries should not be neglected.

16th.   Not more than one horse should be kept on a farm and that number is often one too many.   Horses are the most expensive features of the farm.   Land that cannot be ploughed by a tractor had better not be ploughed.   If a horse is to be kept it should be for the love of it only, or for a few rough odd jobs.

17th.   In dressing lands, do not be misled by the notion that artificial manures are sufficient.   The enthusiast, who in a meeting of farmers, stated as his climax that the time would come when all the fertilizer required for a farm could be carried in the vest pocket, was interrupted by a farmer in the back of the room, " Yes, and the crop in the other pocket." The value of artificial fertilizers is very great, but in a supplementary way, either as top dressing or as added for crop foods in ploughed land.   Absolutely necessary humus must be supplied from the barn yard or through the ploughing under of nitrogen crops.

18th.   Do not fall into the error of building a lot of fences.   The cost is vast and the advantage is often nil.   Nothing but the pasture should be fenced, and that with smooth wire mesh, if the old fence requires any improvement.

19th.   When installing plumbing, pay no attention to the statements of the plumber that it won't freeze.   Let no pipes run up on the outside

A WESTON HOMESTEAD

walls or anywhere near them. Provide heating facilities one half larger than your heating engineer specifies. The feeding of the fires will cost no more, as they will be run lower.

20th. The drainage about the farm buildings aside from the sewer should be natural. Lacking a proper porous soil or a proper slope nothing can be done that is satisfactory. These imperative features should be sought in the first place, and all will come right.

21st. In obtaining a country place inevitable disappointment will follow if financial profit is the first consideration, because no man will make enough to satisfy him, if that is his aim. The first and last and constant

WILLIAMSTOWN WATERS

THE PIONEER HOMESTEAD — CONCORD

COMPARING RABBITS

PEPPERELL WATERS

feeling should be the joy in the occupations connected with developing and carrying on the farm place. It must be considered as an end worth while in itself, and not as a means to something. If it is not good in itself it is not good at all. If one does not enjoy living it and doing it, one will never get enough out of it. In other words one must carry to the country the mind and heart that will find in the country something to fill both.

FARM REVENUES

THE first revenue derived from a farm was the sum received for an old mowing machine sold for junk. It afterward developed that the machine belonged to a neighbor who had stored it in our barn. Revenue sometimes arises from the least expected quarters and is as often lacking from those quarters which were supposed likely to produce it. Potatoes are a mainstay to keep or to sell. Sweet corn is a delusion without a prearranged market. Sometimes it can be sold to a cannery on a contract. Seed raised for nurseries is sometimes a source of revenue, but it cannot do well except in very clean fields, quite free from weeds. At least this applies to grain. It is often possible by careful selection and sorting to secure moderate quantities of seed that is salable in the spring. It is much better to raise most of one's seed, because then one is sure of its freshness. Hay is a bad revenue producer, because it saps the life of the farm to sell it. It should all be fed out on the place. Grains, of course, can never be raised for sale, to advantage, in New England. Eggs from early pullets are profitable, and so are chickens raised very early. Garden products started in a hothouse may often be disposed of to advantage, as such things are rare in the country and there is a considerable number of summer residents who will take them.

Main crops are not for the eastern farmer. He derives his revenue from a great many things; the garden, hennery, orchard, wood lot, a little here and a little there. The exceptions to this statement have mostly been noted above.

PICTURE-MAKING EXPERIENCES

WHEN we visited the William Cullen Bryant place, in Cummington, the day was bright and sweet with sunshine, and the air crisp with the first touch of autumn. The homestead which he loved so much is now vacant. The view from it is very extensive, sweeping for many leagues over the Berkshire hills. The location must be lofty. Back of the dwelling, really coming up to it, in an intimate way, was a splendid wood of pines. Just beyond the farm buildings one entered under the dappled maple shadows (p. 107). About the lawn were fine elms. We could easily understand Bryant's love of trees, and how it continually crept into his poems. We sat down, in a row, at the edge of the porch, and read two or three of his finest appreciations of the natural world. The silence and absence of any living thing about us added much to the effectiveness of the occasion. We knew that the spirit which loved these surroundings was in harmony with our own.

On "A Norfolk Farm Lane" (p. 136) we found a most unusual place. It exemplified the attraction of an independent enterprise, in the old days, which had everything under its own roof. It appears that an early settler had understood vineyarding, and had arranged his basement in a fashion found in some quarters of France. There was a sub-cellar. A huge wine press, worked by a horse going around and around, was installed there, and the great depth and massive stone work showed a feeling for permanency. How little we know what is within doors as we pass by these old dwellings. The rooms of the house were paneled in an interesting way and the location was in every way attractive.

A FRAMINGHAM CAUSEWAY

SWIFT WATER—RUTLAND—PETERSHAM

In Ashfield there is an old embankment, like a moraine, which impounds the lake shown on page 144. A path is worn in the center of the embankment, and on each side are wonderfully beautiful birches with their salmon-colored bark, and lusty large growth. It is a spot much to be sought for on summer days, because a gentle breeze almost always moves across here and the outlook feeds the imagination.

We love the old roadside watering places where drives were arranged so that one passed over little fords, by the sides of the main road (p. 175), for watering the horses. In the early days a long continued " dry spell " was bad for wheels as their spokes tended to rattle. It was bad for the horses' feet, as they became too dry and hard. Travelers were always glad to drive into a brook and wait for a few moments, while the horses drank their fill and wheel and hoof were well soaked. There was even an opportunity to eat luncheon, or, as they used to say, " take a snack."

" The Lynn Marshes " as seen on page 180, remind one of the days of the " Saugus Navy Yard." In the earlier days it was of the utmost importance to work sloops up stream as far as possible, because, in the absence of railroads, and even of roads worthy the name, there was a tendency to form a market at the height of tidewater. It is said that sloops were built at main points where now a row boat would hardly pass, owing to the silting up of old water ways. Laden sloops were taken up at high tide and allowed to strand at low tide. The effect on some of the north sea marshes must have been equal to the effect in Holland where one sees vessels apparently in the midst of the land. On the Saugus River it is said that there was a dam as early as 1629 and a fishway for alewives has been maintained there ever since. Possibly this is the oldest water power in America.

The Aberjona River in Winchester (p. 72) is one of the streams approachable like English rivers. The bushy banks of most of our streams prevent our getting comfortably near them, and we are, therefore, the more delighted when we find grassy banks and an open growth of shade trees. The region all about Winchester is very attractive. A vision

A SOUTH SHORE DOOR

up the stream at Winchester which shows the stone church (p. 276), has all the charm of mellowness and age that we associate with English village scenes.

There is a very ancient dwelling on the old road from Lexington to Concord (p. 263), which probably shows a condition common to many an

WINCHESTER WATERS

CONCORD BRIDGE

WATER LIGHTS—ADAMS

"OLD ENGLAND"—WINCHESTER

early house. The somewhat flat roof, which almost never appeared in the earliest period, generally indicates that the roof lines were carried up by raising the side walls, and at the same time the effect was to flatten the roof. Second story rooms were obtained in this manner, but picturesqueness was lost. This house has wonderful old panels, and that very obvious appearance of never having been dealt with, in its larger rooms, that always appeal to the collector. The overarching elm is rendered more beautiful by a series of small burls, like knobs, covering the main trunk, and many branches. These burls were much used, when on maple and oak trees, for the forming of bowls. The grain of the wood was very beautiful, but the object of the settlers in using it was to obtain material that would not split. This tree is a fine sample of what is often called the rooftree, by confounding this term with the ridgepole, which is the true rooftree.

On page 264 is a bit of the old Connecticut trail running from Weston through Wayland. The residence is the summer home of an artist who has allowed the house to blend itself with the foliage in a subtle fashion.

There is evidently a rabbit trade on between the children sitting on hutches (p. 268). The little girl at the center obviously has the prize animal, and she is the cynosure of neighboring eyes. It would almost seem as if the rabbit was especially created for the delectation of children. Its docility and adaptability make it a pet, better even than a dog, in some particulars. Of course no dog lover would admit for a moment that the finer intelligence and affection of his dog would place it in the same class with any other pet whatsoever.

THE FUTURE OF MASSACHUSETTS

A GOOD citizen will naturally ask himself whether he can be serviceable in making the future of Massachusetts, not safe for democracy, but safe for developing humanity.

OLD INN—NORTH BROOKFIELD

We were at the polls the other day and certainly we felt no pride in democracy. It is, indeed, the best form of government if intelligence accompanies it; otherwise is it not the very worst form of government? Somehow we must get before our people images of beauty. They must become accustomed to seeing fair outlines, because education is mostly a matter of the eye, with the average man. If we can establish regions, where no unsightliness reigns for a mile, could anything promise better for our future? There are districts where special efforts, in sanitation and health education, are being attempted, with the idea of forming model

ELM BY THE RIBBON ROAD—ROYALSTON

A HINGHAM LANE

A HATFIELD DOOR

communities in these respects. But the mind of a man cannot be normal unless it can feed on something worth looking at. There are towns like Lancaster, for instance, where the tree warden is instructed to guard and foster the beauties of the roadside, and more and more that highly important action is being followed up in other towns. There is nothing as yet, however, that prevents a citizen from choosing ugliness rather than beauty in his dwelling as well as his grounds.

People are very apt to stand on their constitutional rights when they wish to do nothing. We remember a notably indolent person who, when offered a job, replied tartly that the Constitution of the United States guaranteed him the right to work or not as he pleased. Of course, the Constitution guaranteed him no such thing, but freedom is, in the thought of many, freedom to be indolent or to do poorly and slackly what ought to be done well. There is no way of reaching such persons. They are self-punished, but their punishment does not reform them, at least now. Example, therefore, is the only teacher, and the owner of country acres who is careful to see that his quarter mile of road is treated in an esthetic manner, is doing for the community as much as he can, perhaps.

Massachusetts has the advantage of age. Her roads are largely constructed, as well as her established culture features. She has traditions of decency. She has many excellent examples of honest dealing with nature so as to bring her beauties to the fore, rather than to mask them and kill them. There is wealth, and a long experience of good and bad methods. There is a militant minority eager for the beautifying of the state.

Of course we shall not have a thoroughly beautiful state without understanding that even external beauty must rest on the character of the people. A sense of permanence and strength must be in the character. Otherwise how shall we avoid the shingled candle extinguishers and the gimcrack ornaments, which are placed on dwellings? Unless there is repose in a man's nature reposeful architecture will not result. A fair countryside is the consequence of sympathy with nature, so that she is led rather than thwarted and distorted. After a while we find that it is not newness and

A SCITUATE DOOR

freshness that we want in our homesteads, but a blending in color, form and material, that makes them a part of the landscape in which they stand.

We are learning that we have done many unnecessary things; that we have dragged in material from afar which was not so good as that which lay all around us. We have adopted exotic forms, and such designs as lead one to suppose that the dwelling is temporarily set down where it is, rather than that it grew there out of the needs of the place.

THE TRACERY OF MAY—LANCASTER

GARDENS AT PITTSFIELD

FISHERMAN'S LUCK

KING HOOPER HOUSE APPROACH—DANVERS

Our farm papers and magazines are not living up to their opportunity in setting before the country people the restful, low, solid forms of structures. We have of late been placing classical libraries in our New England villages. Their roofs are always pitched too low and are bound to cause loss to the contents of the edifices together with decay and disintegration of the buildings. We have supposed it incumbent upon us to follow a style. One cannot say that an ancient stone farmhouse in France or England has a style. It is better that there should be no mark that speaks loudly of design. Strength and comfort and utility are to be satisfied first, and not an ornament should be added for its own sake.

It will be a long day before these facts are felt by all the people. Still, they will be felt perhaps in a hundred years, and we shall get back to a point where we were two hundred years ago. It will be a distinct advance, for the building of that time was based upon the needs rather than upon the uneducated pretensions of the owner.

A like principle goes with landscape features. It may be necessary, in the case of important thoroughfares, to fill up the valleys and cut down the hills. In the case of side roads, however, and the banks of brooks, and the contour of building sites, very much happier results are achieved by taking the world as we find it. For instance, we remember forty years ago a country place was bought by a wealthy man, who proceeded at once to wall in the brook, from end to end, through his farm. It was not a brook that required imprisonment. Its banks were far more beautiful before than after the supposed improvement. It had formed its own rocky bed and in the process of ages it had its small strands and its steep banks. It was merely walled in with the thought of adding to its beauty!

In the same way thirty years ago a site was smoothed for a house. Ledges were blasted out. Boulders were rolled away. A precise and even surface was secured. There was nothing interesting in the result. There was nothing natural, or comporting with the surrounding landscape. There was no possible advantage. Now we are learning to make use of upcropping rocks and to cease to make over a country.

It is amazing to consider the vast expenditure in fighting natural land-scapes, and making them far worse than they were before.   True art con-sists in taking advantage of conditions.   In the same way we are learning that rows of trees about dwellings, are not as attractive as trees scattered irregularly.

Borrowing the same thought for the gable of the house, that shows through the trees, it is no longer thought necessary to secure a symmetrical gable.   If the windows are placed to balance without, very likely the dwelling is thrown out of harmony within.   Just as we would not want a tree with all limbs alike so we should not seek for country homes with both sides alike.

That these views are borne out in experience is easily demonstrable. Look through any art gallery or at any picture in public or private owner-ship, that has the endorsement of persons of training.   Is it a set and for-mal scene?   Not once in a thousand times.   If the author were to select precise and new dwellings, or masonry fences, as the accessories of the pic-tures in this book, who would look twice at them?   In order to satisfy any artistic feeling at all there must be mellowness and a rounding away of sharp corners.   There must be curves and adaptations.   What nature has taken many ages to accomplish we ought not to change with thoughtless hands.   This is not to say that persons who dwell in marsh lands should not drain their marshes, or that those who dwell in a country of unbroken timber should not clear a space for their dwelling.   But the underlying springs of action are best expressed perhaps by saying that we should work in sympathy with the natural world, and take advantage of every bit of work wrought for us, by the forces of wind and water and vegetation.

As the dust of the earth is availed of by the clouds and the sun to give us the splendors of color overhead, so it is possible for us, by careful adaptation of our own work to what seem the mistakes of nature, to secure results wholly charming and also meeting the needs of the average man.

We were driving home one day and looking into the west.   Slowly there began to marshal themselves feathery bits of cloud, rank on rank, in

MAY ON THE TURNPIKE — MIDDLESEX

THE TIME OF JOY — SUDBURY

A CHARLEMONT COTTAGE—MOHAWK TRAIL

SNOW DECKED—DEDHAM

A LITTLE PATH IN WESTON

delicate color and general symmetry of form. They rose in broad twin
platoons, from a central point, until they covered a third of the sky. We
drew up by the roadside to see this demonstration of glory. It was more

marvelous than that of the burning bush which was not consumed. It indicated a mind in nature that loved and fostered beauty. It formed from dust and mist majestic archangels' wings.

We said within ourselves that this is ever the effort of mind in nature, to bring out beauty from a growing world. It is a world where most remains yet to be done. It is a world, so far as Massachusetts is concerned, with inspiring possibilities. Perhaps the important thing for us to remember is that we are not working alone. There is, of course, always, everywhere a protective power, a stimulating beauty, an effort at revelation, an unfolding of glory in form and color. There is a new life, a changing aspect, a better coming out of a good. There is a latent grandeur in the rock-ribbed world. That we have come so far indicates a majestic and mighty tide of intelligent purpose, to catch up into power and beauty the grasses, the leaves, the stones and the very dust. Just to live, and feel this, is an endless thrill of confidence and joy, and a call to get into step.

It is a time of many laws. Inspirations are better than laws. A sense of the unity of nature, and a recognition of her glorious achievements, apart from us, is the beginning of education. Her best is good enough for this world, or any world, and her best with man's best, is a combination formed only in joy and the love of harmony. We shall find a better world as our eyes are opened.

HIDDEN HOMES

IF we understand the outline of the character of Adam which of course was inspired by the character of the narrator, a great deal of the joy which he got out of life was in having a plot of ground retired, personal and peculiar. On page 219 Cress Brook Road shows a little hidden domain in Norfolk county. It is withdrawn some quarter of a mile from the highway, and while the public is free to drive in on one side and out on the other, the road is practically private. It winds and rises and falls

HOME ARCHES—HOLLISTON

HOMEWARD BOUND—MILLIS-SHERBORN

ELM SHADOWS

DOROTHY PERKINS

and passes an orchard, a meadow, a lake and a wood. The owner, some years since, found and developed the old homestead on a knoll, facing the water, and has a little domain hidden from the world. She will not be aware until she sees this sketch that the author has ever gleaned the charms of her drive. The marvel of such gleaning is that one leaves more behind him than he found, because when one looks upon and enjoys anything, and tells it, the location becomes more worthy in the eyes of those who follow.

Most of the great number of pictorial records made by the author are still unknown to the residents nearest the scenes concerned. Not a few are charming spots never so thought of or at least thought of as purely local by the owners, but now made known broadly through the country. There is in store for many, as the years go on, an agreeable surprise, to find how much some nook or reach, familiar to the owner, has become loved by the general public.

In the Cress Brook Road we have an example in which the views are all near, and the contour is wonderfully beautiful, though there is no distant prospect. It is a hiding place from the storms and the cares and the intrusions of the great world. It is our view that the main purpose of a home is the individual touch, and the charm of personal devotion to a few acres, by which the mind of the owner impresses itself on the landscape about him. It is an expression of his thought, in the curves of the walls, the foliage by the roadside, the grouping of the trees, secured by restraint or stimulus, and all the nameless marks of comfort or taste or enterprise, resulting from a mellow acquaintance with that particular section of God's earth.

THE VARIETY OF ROOF OUTLINES

WE have shown here and there the remarkably large number of roof styles which were used, all of them within a century, and all of them good. The so called monitor roof which rises in a kind of clear story, is here and there found through the 18th century. The great three story houses of the latter part of that century with their four chimneys, did not slant the roofs as much as in the earlier part of the same century. They secured a roomy dwelling but at the expense of picturesqueness and weatherproof construction. We also have the gambrel of which Holmes wrote:

> " Gambrel, gambrel, let me beg
> You'll look at a horse's hinder leg,
> First great angle above the roof,
> That's the gambrel, hence gambrel roof."

We were slow to bring in this style and did not long continue to follow it. It is now being revised to a very great extent, and in certain sections of New England even the barns are constructed in this manner. Then, beginning with the pointed Gothic gable, which came in again in the Gothic revival of 1830, we proceed to the pavilion type, the so-called French roof type, and the broken roof, where various levels meet in picturesque confusion, and which belongs to no particular order of architecture. That style in which the second story window rises through the plate and becomes a kind of half dormer, so beautiful in England, when thatched, has been attempted here occasionally. Between the houses of wood, brick and stone arising out of our wealth of material, good American domestic architecture shows a wide and pleasing variety, nowhere better seen than in old Massachusetts. The roofs which slope four ways from a great central chimney, the roofs which have their pairs of chimneys at each end connected by a straight brick tie, the lean-to, the bow roof, the decked roof, and a great variety of combinations, exhibit an interesting record of tastes or needs.

A COLERAINE ARCH

INDEX

297